AF377685

Goin' Down the Road with Robert Frank

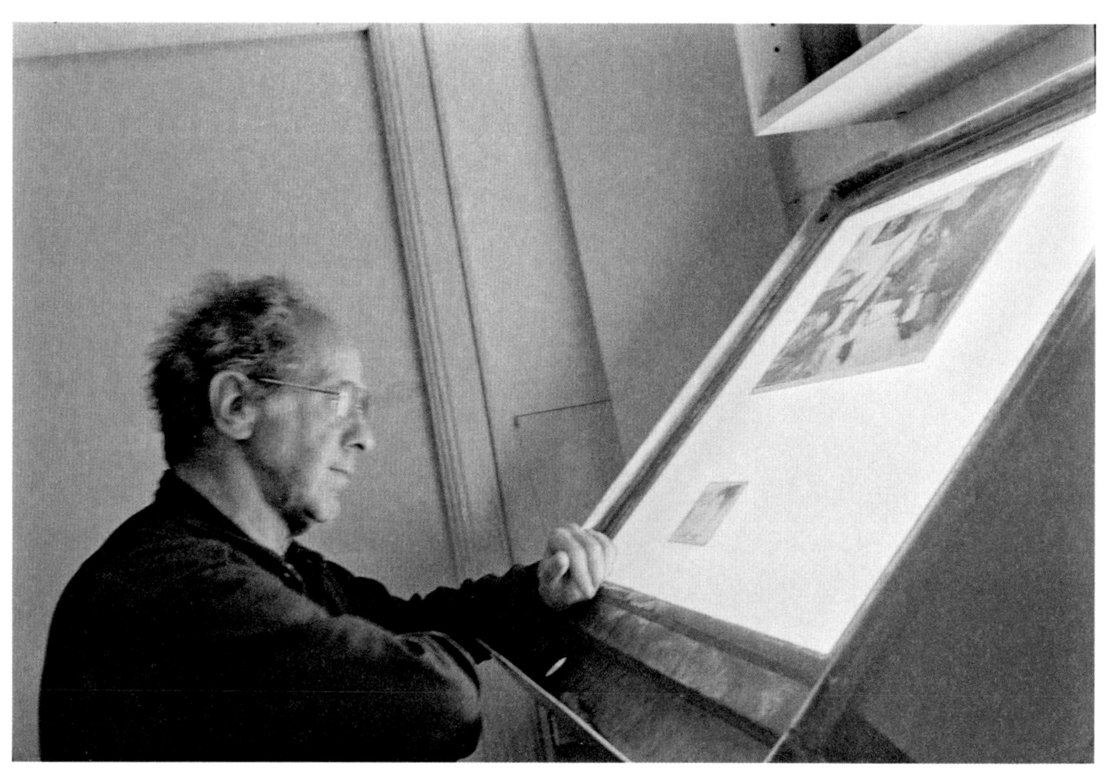

Robert Frank in my darkroom, NYC, 1988

BRIAN GRAHAM

Goin' Down the Road
with Robert Frank

Introduction by Ai Weiwei

Steidl

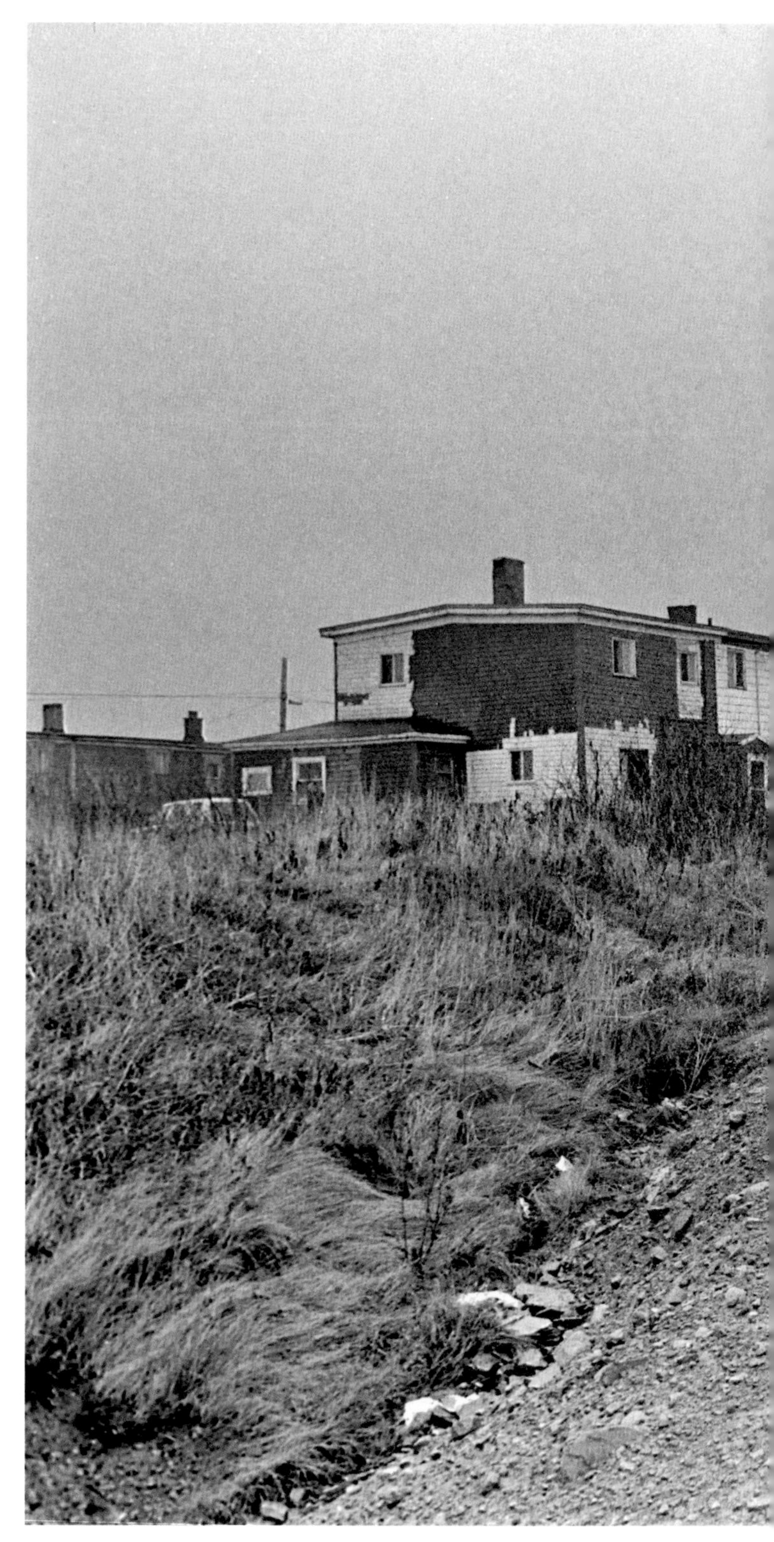

Scouting location for *Candy Mountain*,
Glace Bay, Nova Scotia, 1985

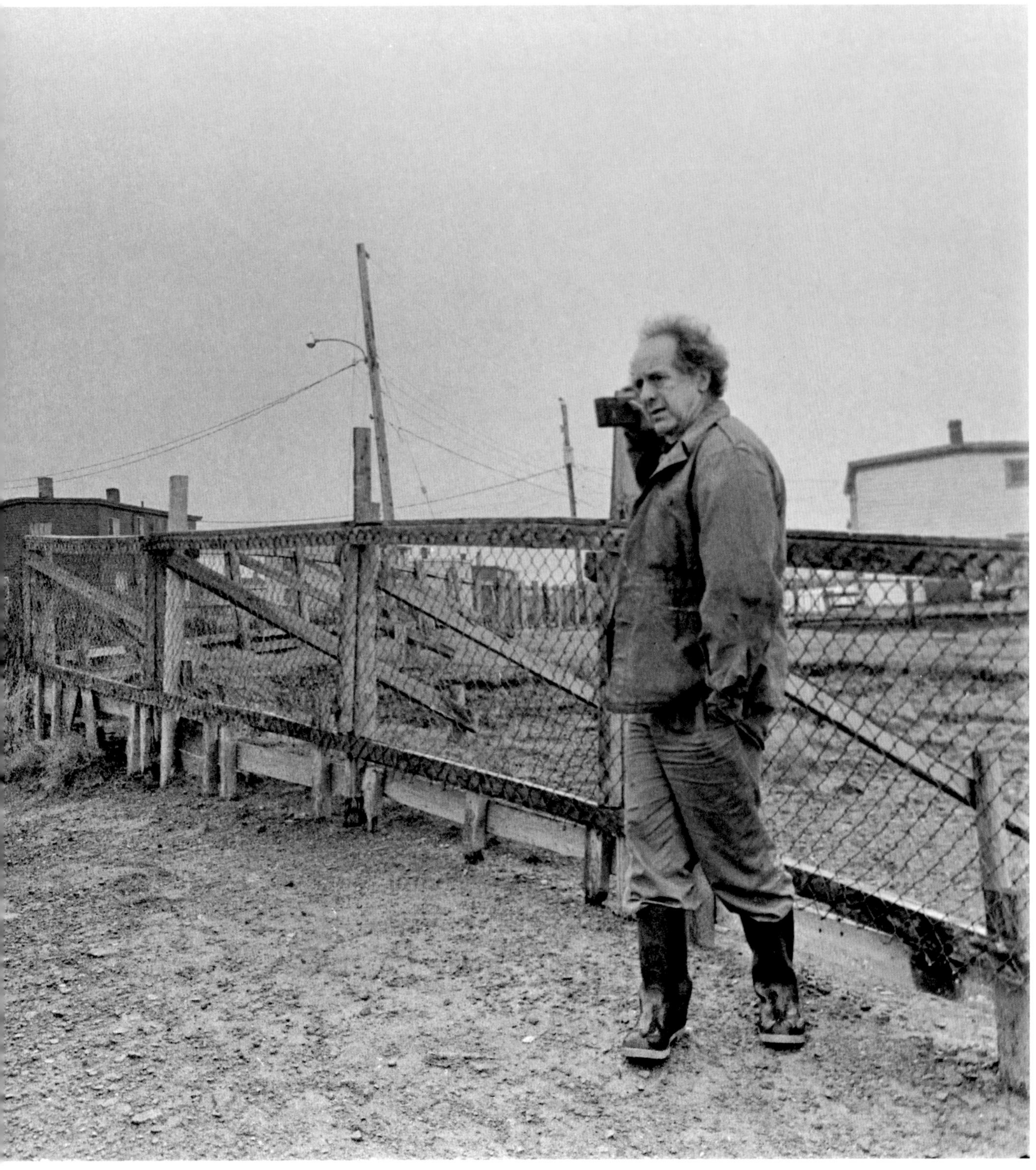

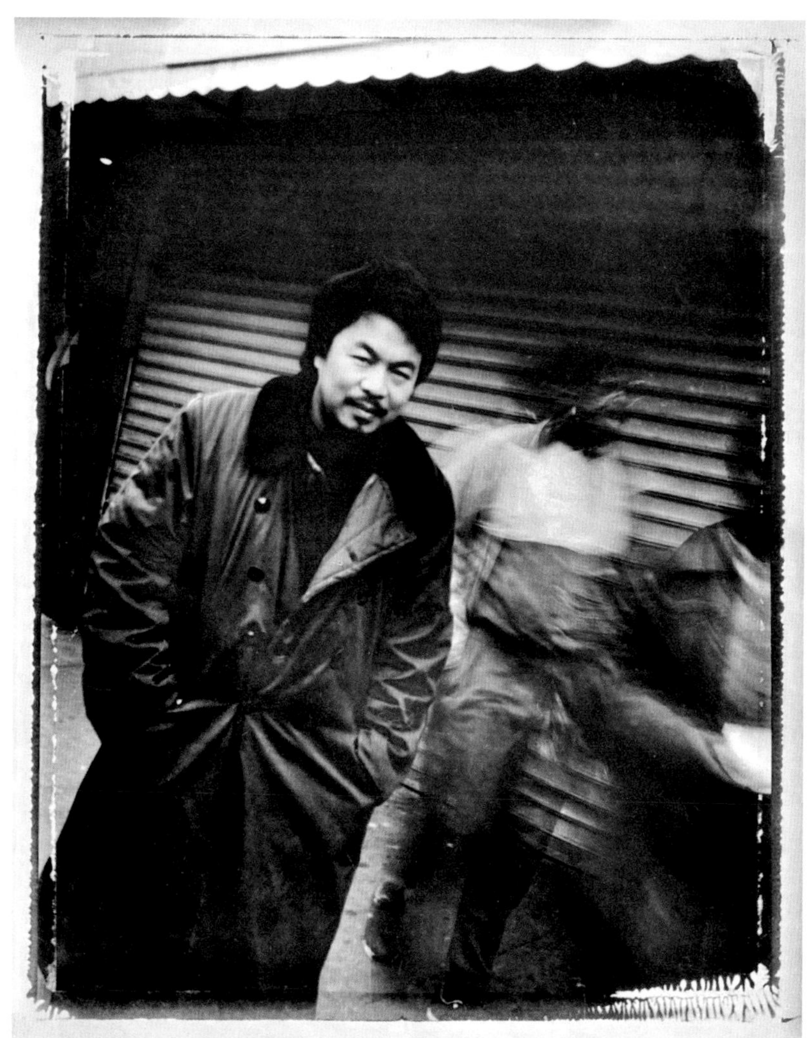

Ai Weiwei, St. Mark's Place, NYC, 1991

Individual or collective understandings of reality – be it individual reality, social reality, political environment, or history – can only be completely achieved through a certain mode of expression. Photography is an important way to solidify this expression. Our perception of the reality of the past, if detached from visual images and records, would be illusory.

Based on this conclusion, there are at least two important elements in photography; here I am talking about both still photography and cinematography. The first element is that photography accurately and mercilessly records an event of a certain moment and a visual fragment, which is used to explain our memory, what has once happened and how we once were. This is an important basis, without which our understanding of the past would be blurred or simply wrong. Secondly, the "evidence" of these memories, if we regard it as a cultural phenomenon, is crucial to the meaning of human existence today because our life still needs to be re-examined and redefined. The re-examination and redefinition would remain muddled if there were no literature, art, photography, and cinematography. We can thus conclude that we do not know who we are until we see the concrete fragments of our memories. Photography provides us with indispensable reserves of ore for our memories, which can be smelted and cast again.

Brian is a friend of mine from the early nineties. We have known each other for almost thirty years, but a lot of memories have been erased during the years. When he got in touch with me again and sent me his photography book on Robert Frank, it brought back memories of the eighties and early nineties and the culture of the Lower East Side in New York. I recognized some people in his photography whom I knew but was not familiar with. The most familiar face is Allen Ginsberg. I met Robert Frank and some other frequent guests at Allen's place. These photos brought me back to the scenes of that period; Robert had that familiar shirt on, which he wore all the time and almost felt like the only shirt he had.

Brian gave me the impression of a very casual person. In the East Village towards the end of the eighties and the beginning of the nineties, there was no lack of casual and idle people. Both Brian and I belonged to that type, which means that we could loll anywhere along the pavement, aimlessly have a chat, or walk in any direction. Randomness and inadvertency were the reality of our life at that time. We had no concrete idea of where we were and where we were heading. I was not aware of where I came from, what kind of storms I went through, what pushed me to those islands of New York, what was the force behind it. Being young, this randomness and aimlessness is the synonym of freedom and the main characteristic of Brian's photography. When he took the photos that we see here, we did not know what he was doing, where he was, or why these photos were taken. It was exactly this randomness and aimlessness that explains the power of photography and the inexplicable motivation of photography.

Through chemical means in the old days and digital means nowadays, photography, though never a part of the real, is a mode of expression that is closest to reality. Seemingly casual and random photos can reach a level of saturation and power that is often more consequential than the photos with carefully designed and composed light, color, and narrative; all human efforts pale by comparison with the manifestation of nature and seem a bit clumsy, narrow, limited, and too eager for a quick success.

I am very happy to see Brian's photography. It's like a stone sunk to the bottom of the water surfaces and brings me back to thirty years ago and all that I experienced at that time.

Ai Weiwei

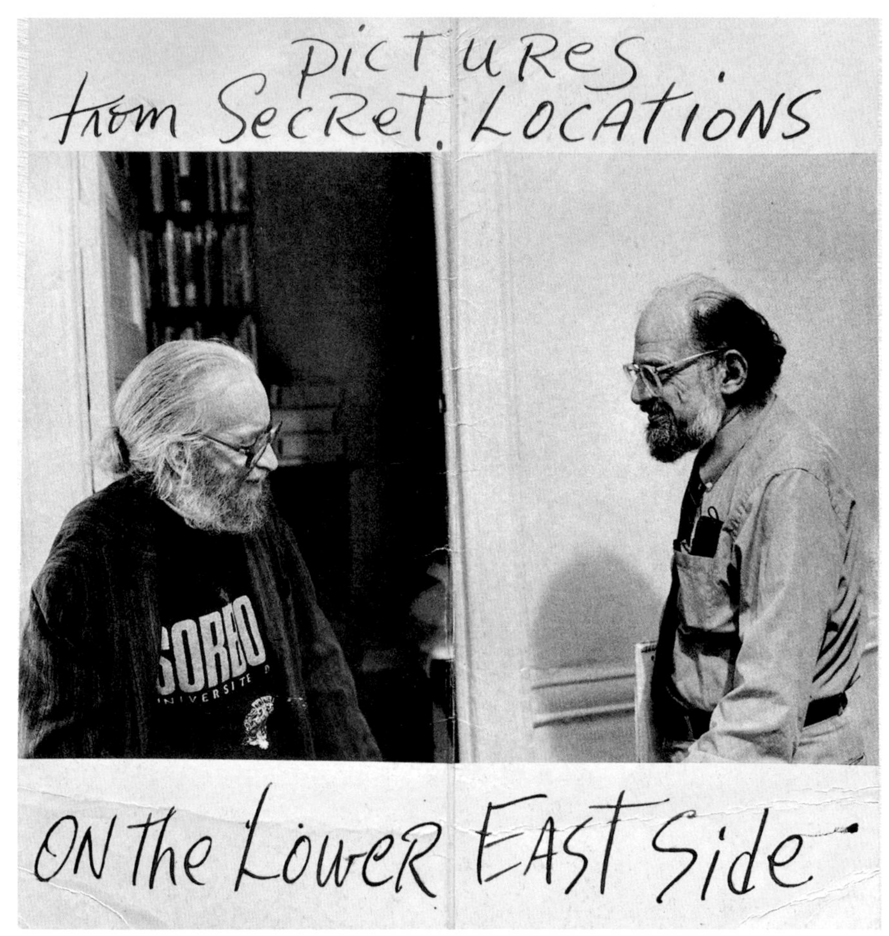

Harry Smith and Allen Ginsberg on East 12th Street, 1985

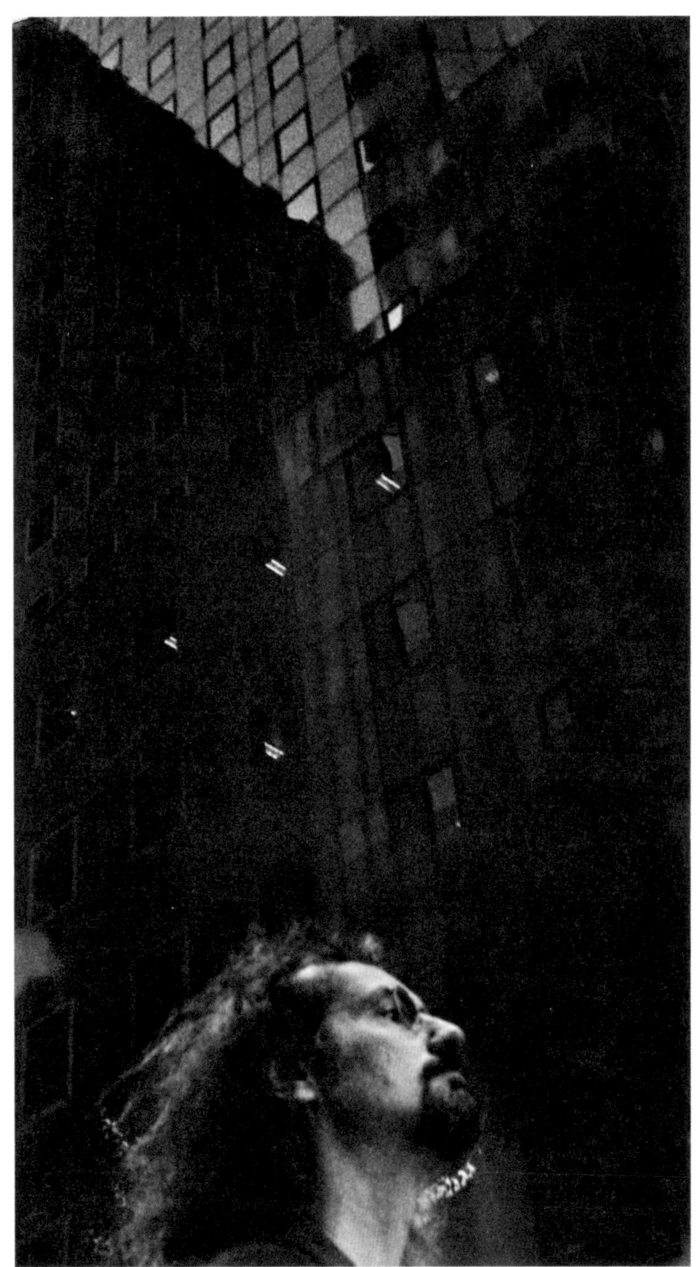

Photo by Romy Karbjinski

GOIN' DOWN THE ROAD WITH ROBERT FRANK
My travels with The Chief

Robert helped me beat the devil with Polaroid Type 665 positive/negative film. The Chief had respect and interest in people who took to the road and returned with a good story to tell. *Goin' Down the Road* was a Canadian road film by Donald Shebib that Robert liked. The story started out with two Cape Breton buddies leaving the island to seek factory work in Toronto. By the time I caught up with Robert I had been working on oil rigs in 1976 and '77. First it was Grand Prairie and Red Deer, Alberta, then offshore near Sable Island and the Labrador Sea. I was in need of transition and Robert recognized it. He liked my story of growing up in Glace Bay. He listened and told me, "That's obvious, you have to go back there and photograph where you came from." The next time I visited Robert in Mabou Mines, he had been to New York and brought back a Polaroid Model 195 for me to try out in The Bay.

I arrived in New York 1981 at Robert's invitation – before comfort had reached the Lower East Side. That first block of Bleecker Street on the Bowery seemed forgotten and abdicated to a bygone era. Living next to Robert were the photographers Ed Grazda, Paco Grande and Gary Hill who I got to know quite quickly. It seemed they split from the artistic conventions of the time and this place allowed it, meaning that the Lower East Side was completely different from the rest of the city. I worked in and out of the darkroom with Robert for over ten years. There were special moments when Robert confided in me. It could be some encounter with a neighbor in Mabou or any past or present friendship – Ed Grazda, Allen Ginsberg or any one of our mutual friends. Traveling with Robert was like walking on a swinging suspension bridge and that's how I liked it. Robert was a changed person when he resided in Mabou; he once told someone that moving there had saved his life. The man was imagined, felt, witnessed, needed, trusted.

Brian Graham

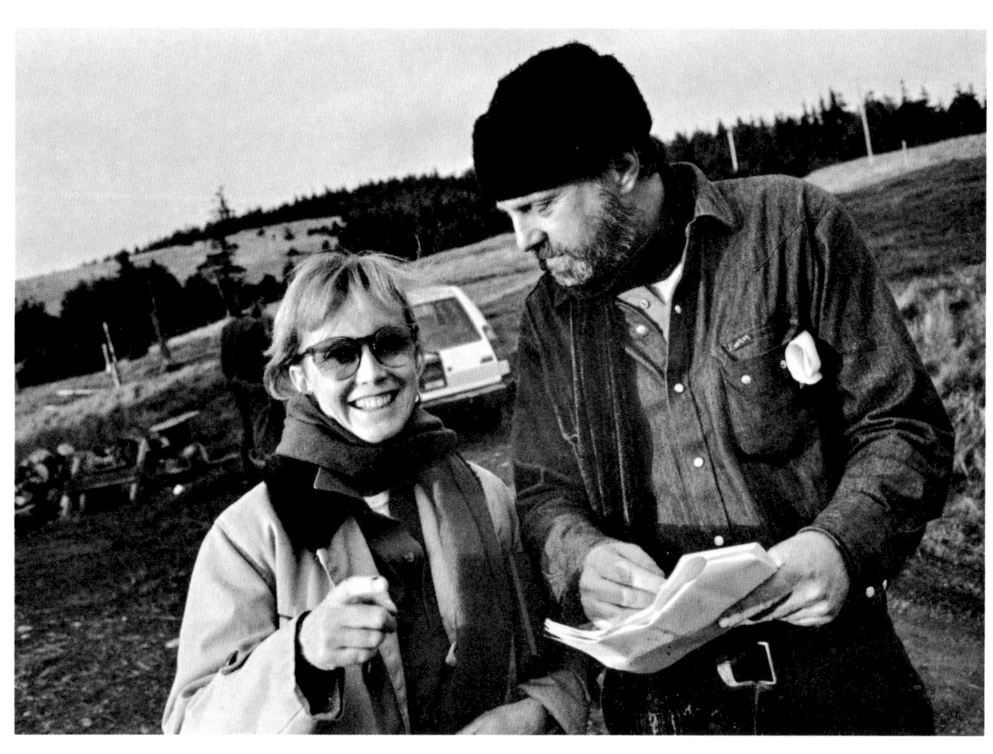

Bulle Ogier and Rudy Wurlitzer,
Candy Mountain, Mabou, 1985

IT STILL DOES GO ON

May 2021

These days often find me thinking and remembering Robert Frank. We traveled together in many ways, including a film that evolved on its own without a conceptual plan. Robert remains inside me and I always refer to his presence when launching another project.

For Robert, less often leads to more and more to less. It didn't matter if he was sitting in a crowded room or drifting inside the solitude of a generous display of nature. He was often penetrating in his remarks and observations, no matter the social cost. I salute and revere him for standing strong in the pursuit of truth. Alas, so it goes or might have gone, or doesn't even if it still does.

Rudy Wurlitzer

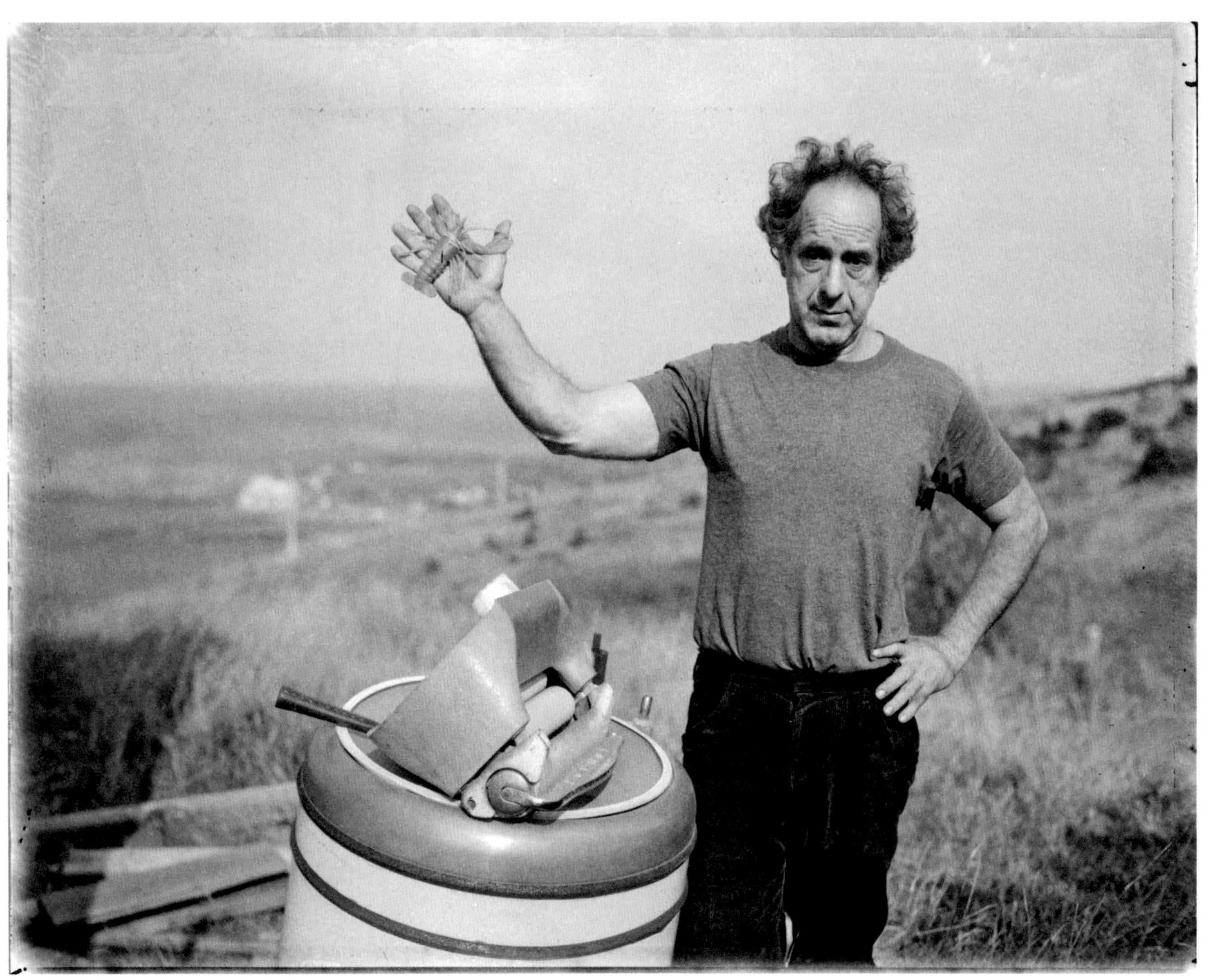

Mabou, Cape Breton, 1979

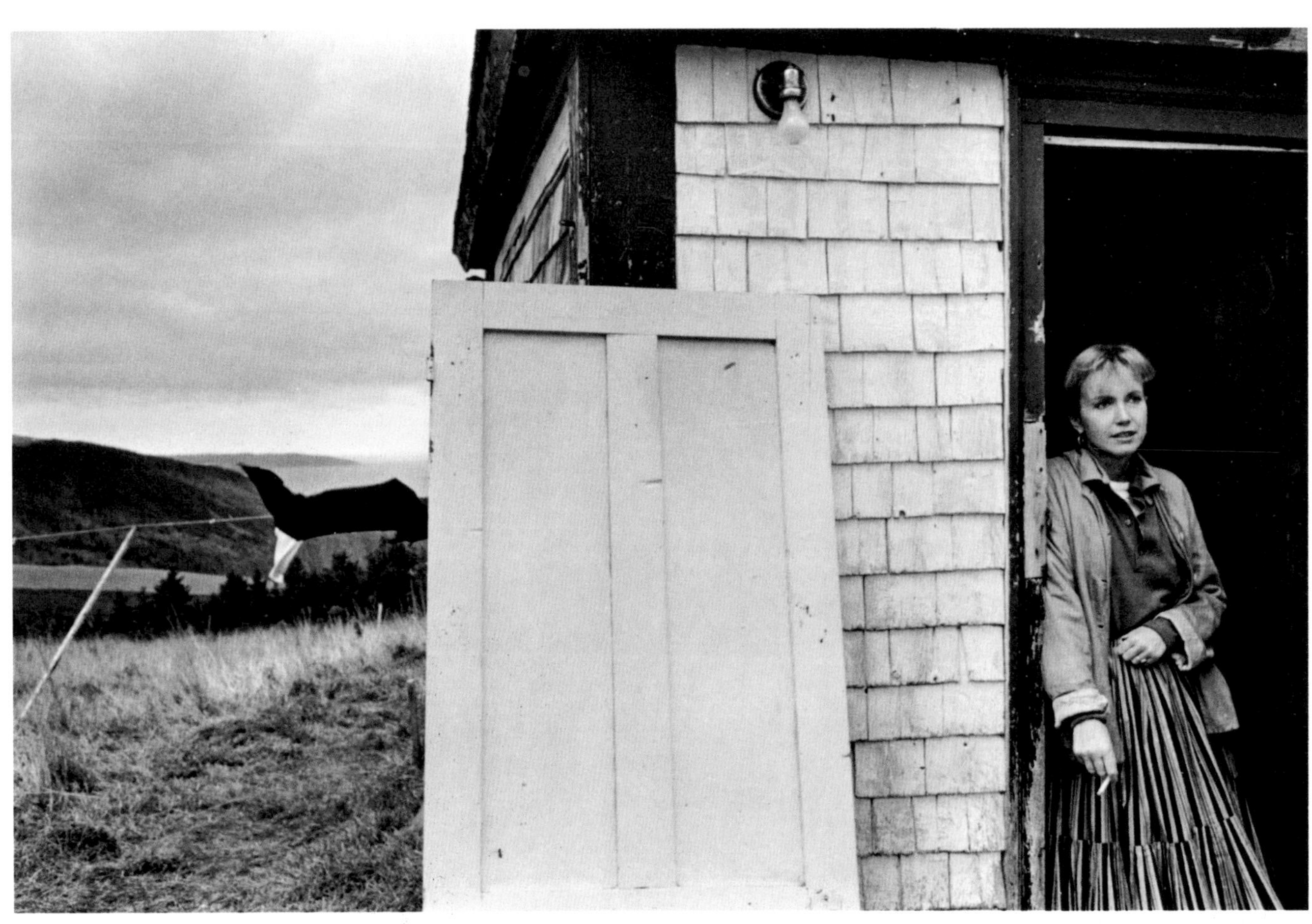

Bulle Ogier as Cornelia in *Candy Mountain*, Mabou, 1985

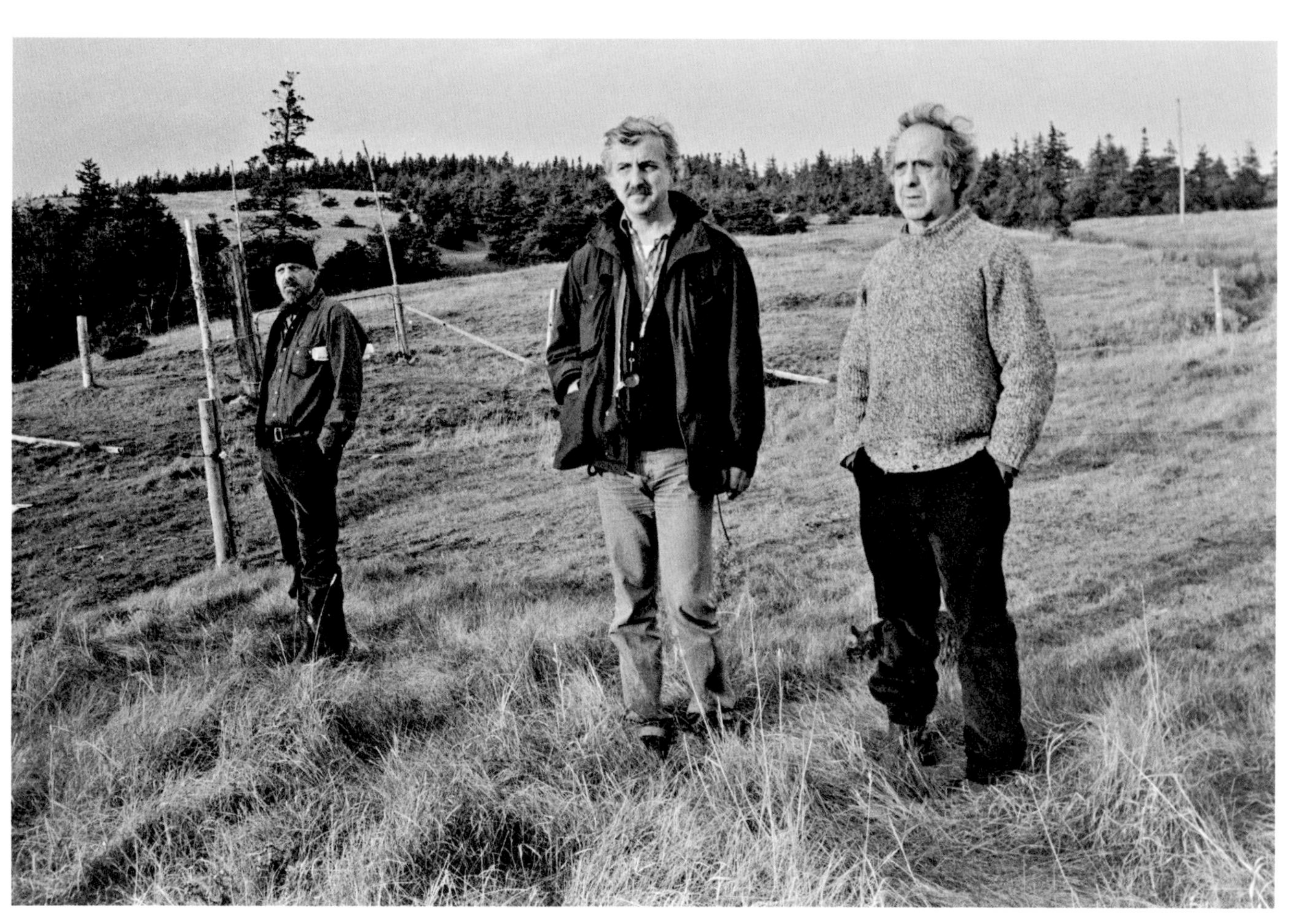

Rudy Wurlitzer, Pio Corradi and Robert on the set of *Candy Mountain*, Mabou Mines, Nova Scotia, 1985

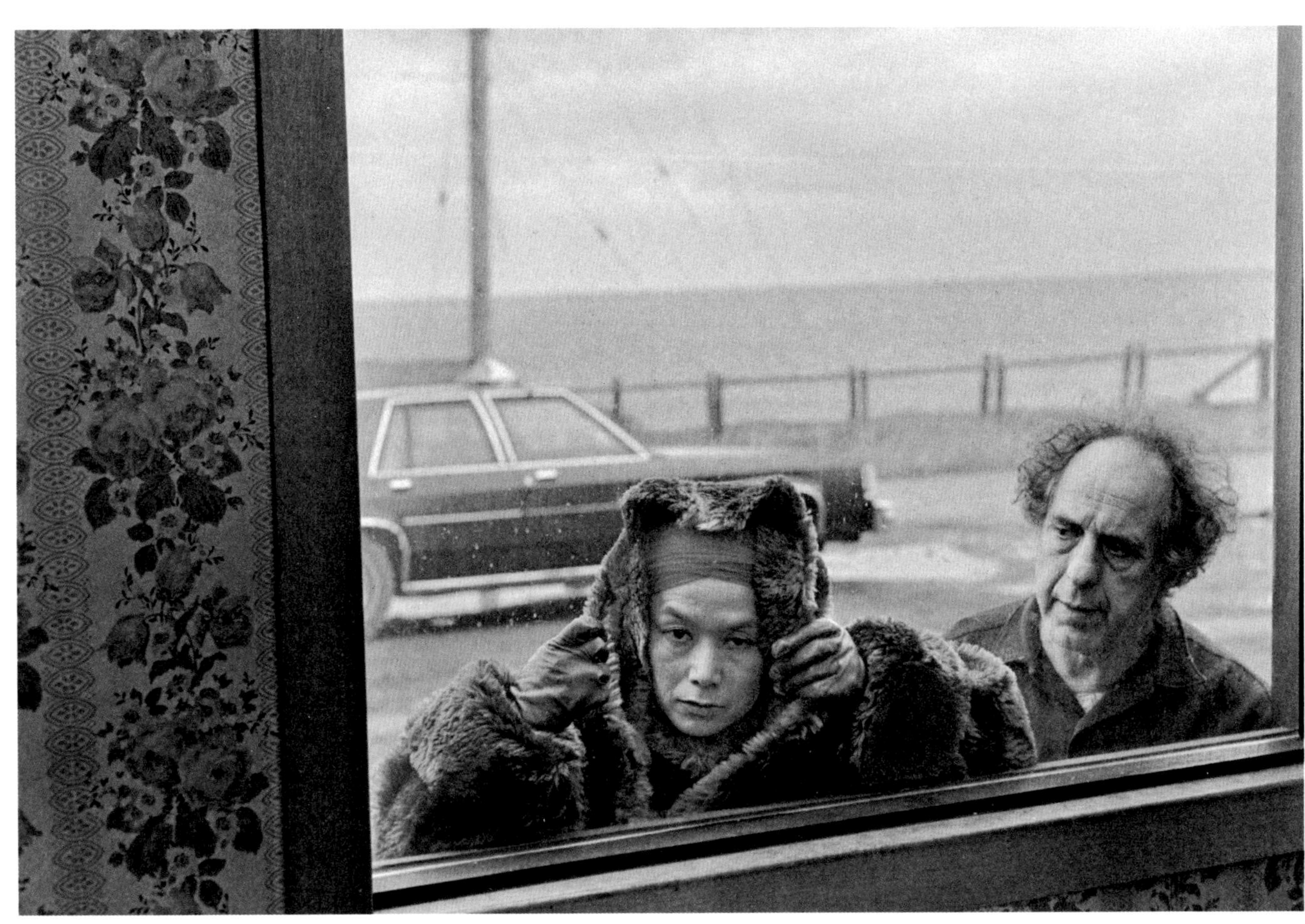

Robert directing Kazuko Oshima on the set of *Candy Mountain*,
Glace Bay, Nova Scotia, 1985

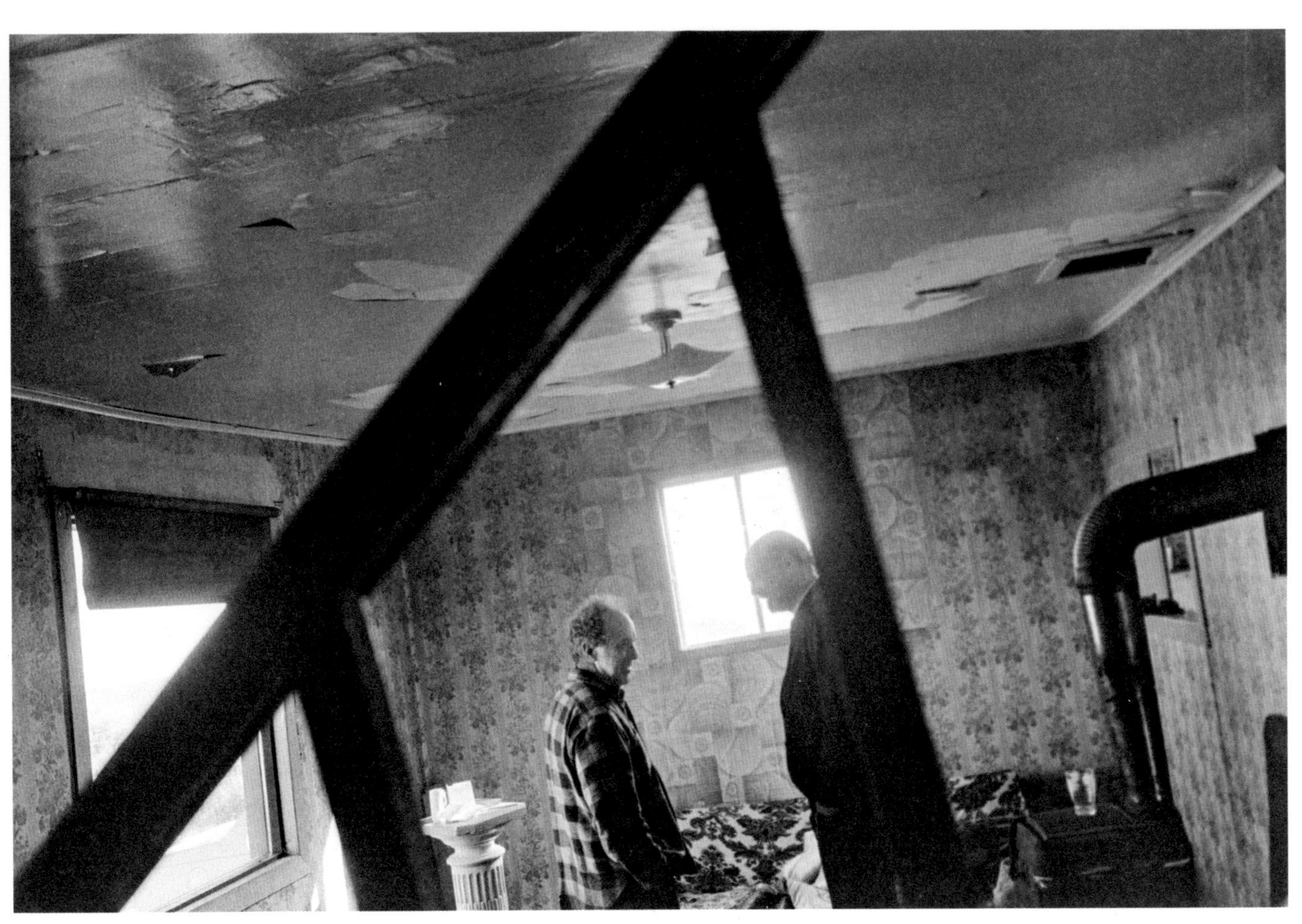

Robert and Rudy Wurlitzer co-directing *Candy Mountain*, Glace Bay, Nova Scotia, 1985

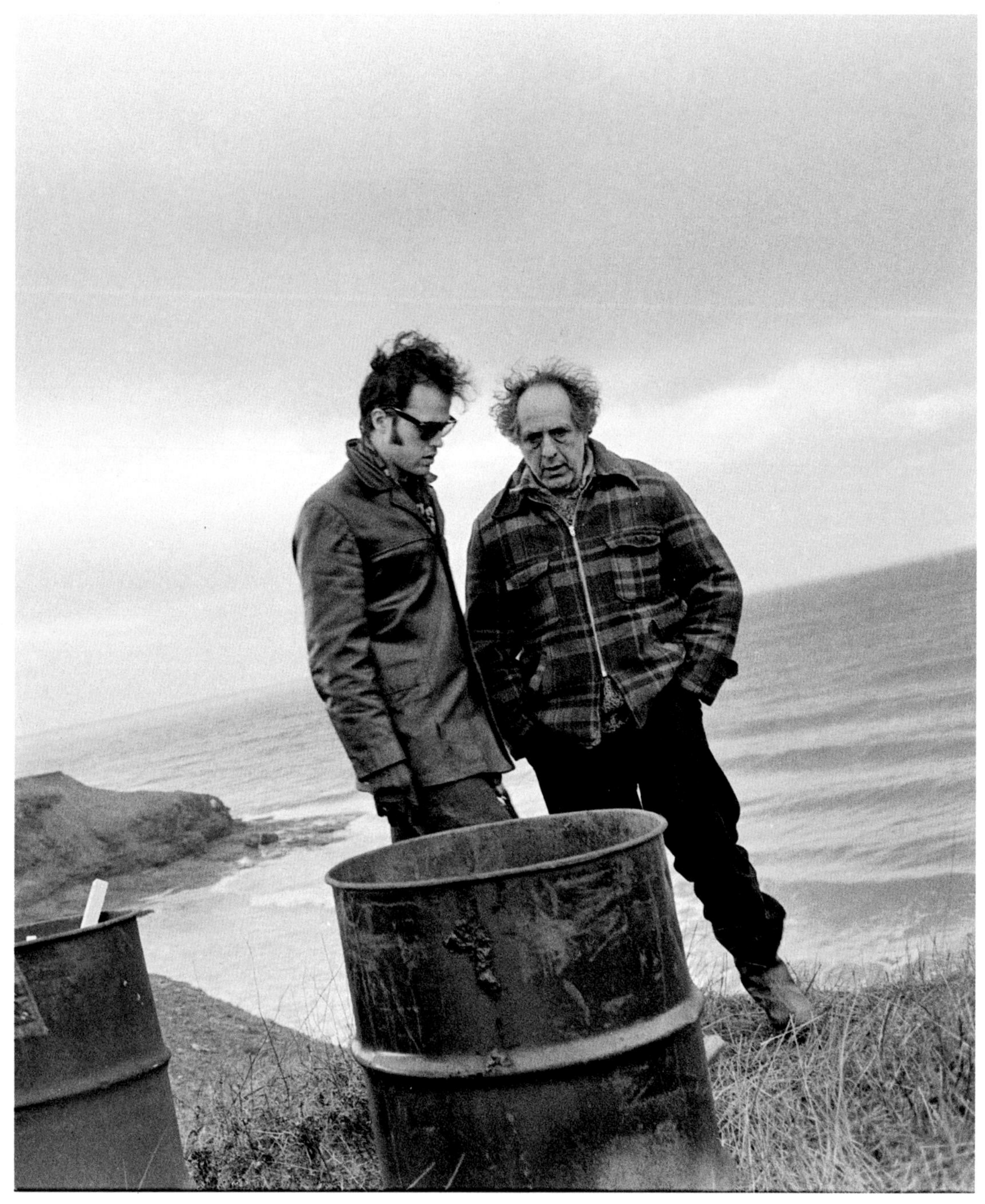

Kevin J. O'Connor and Robert on the set of *Candy Mountain*, Glace Bay, Nova Scotia, 1985

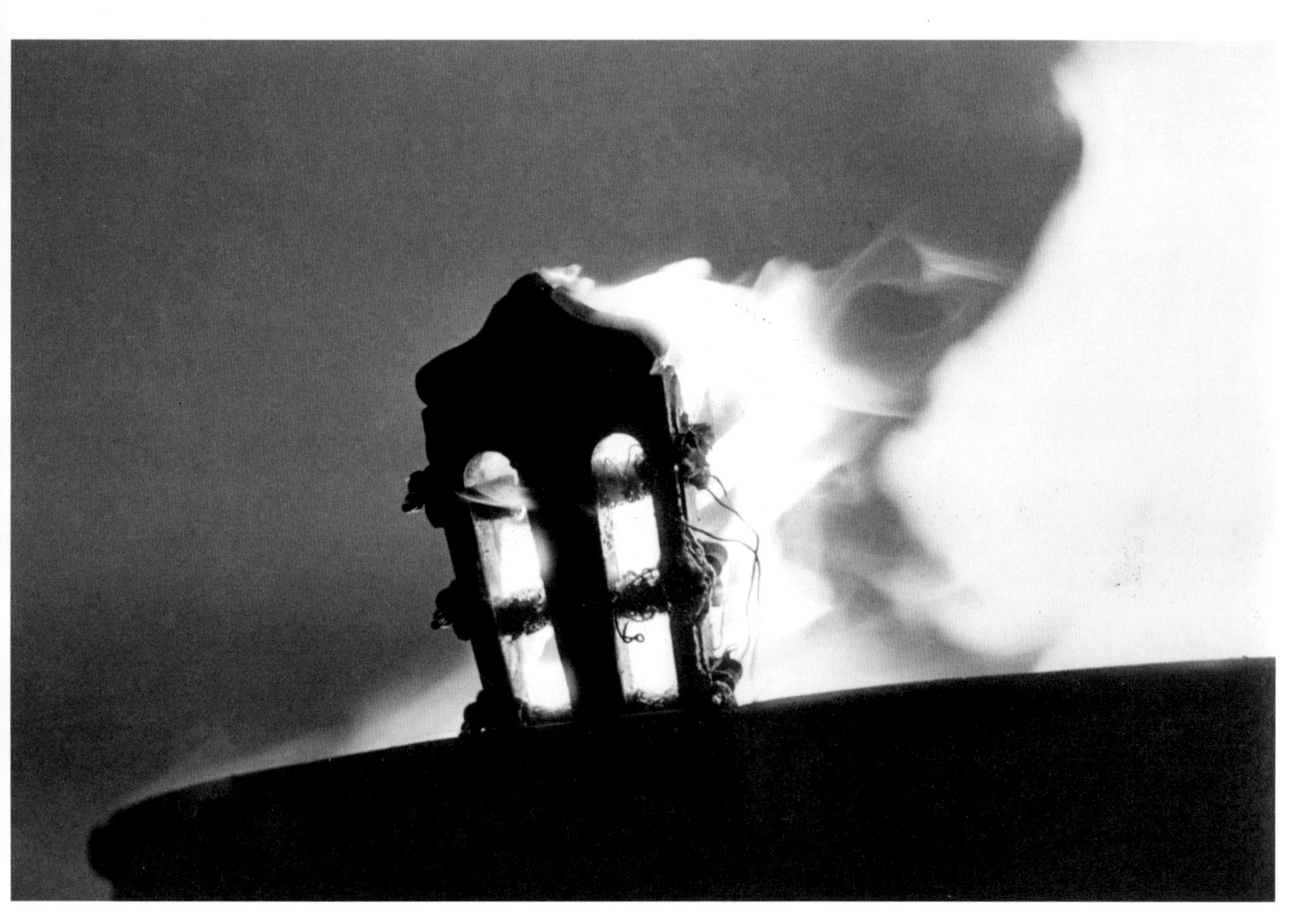

Elmore Silk´s legendary guitars go up in smoke

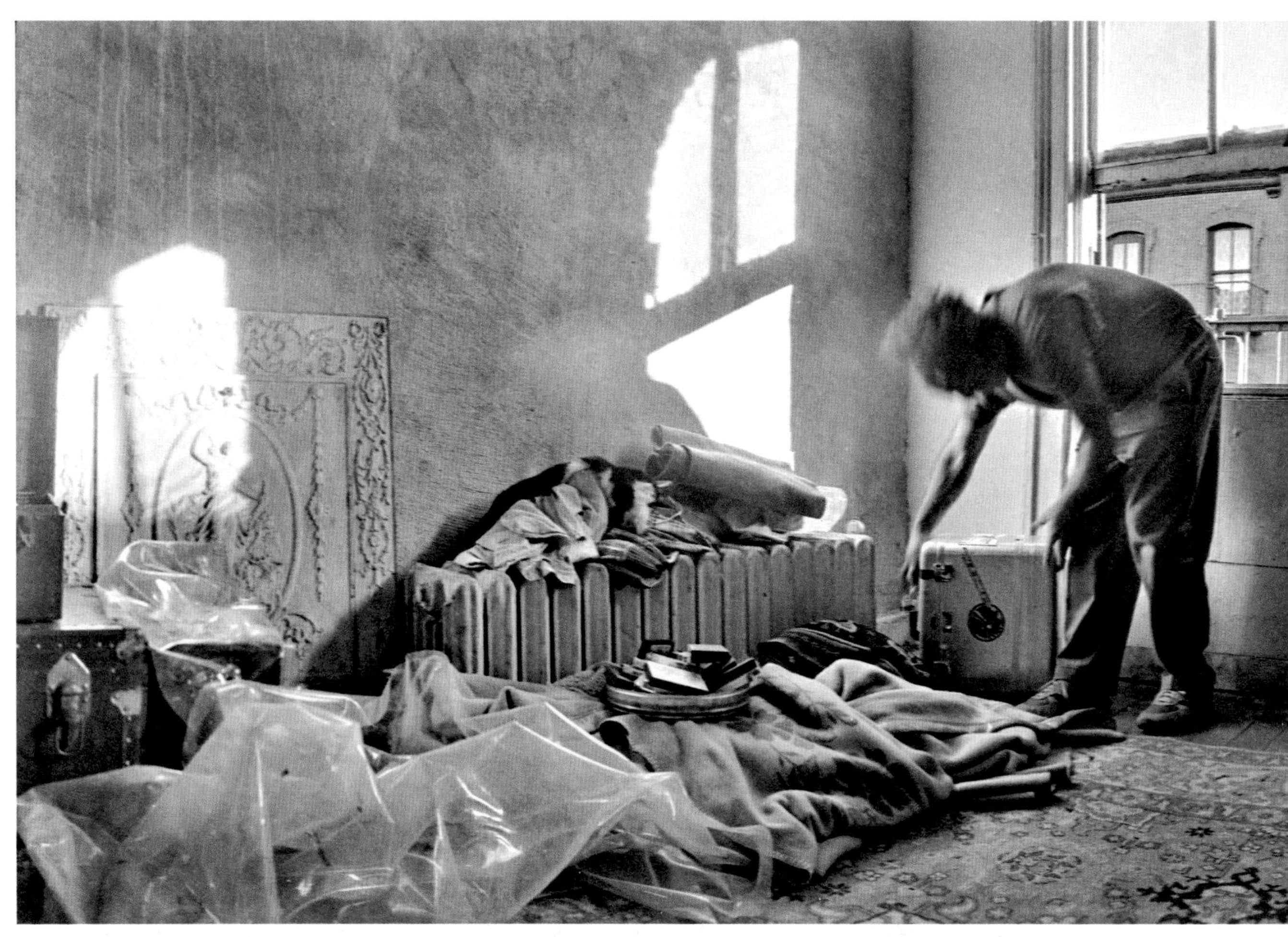

Preparing for travel to Mabou, 7 Bleecker Street, NYC, 1983

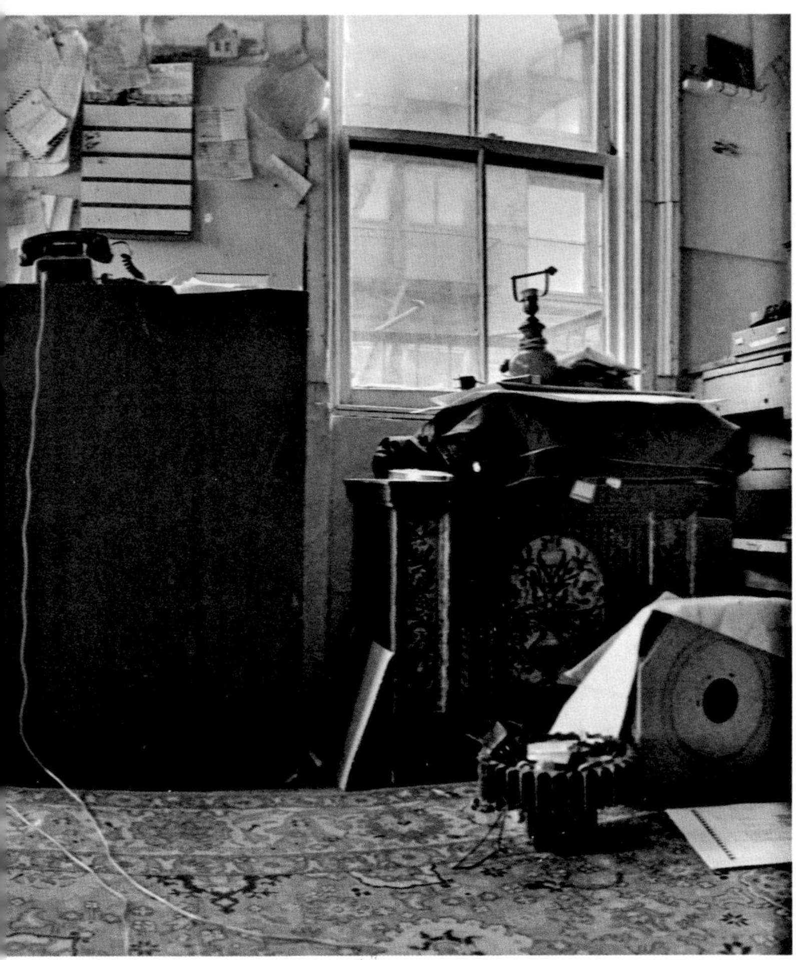

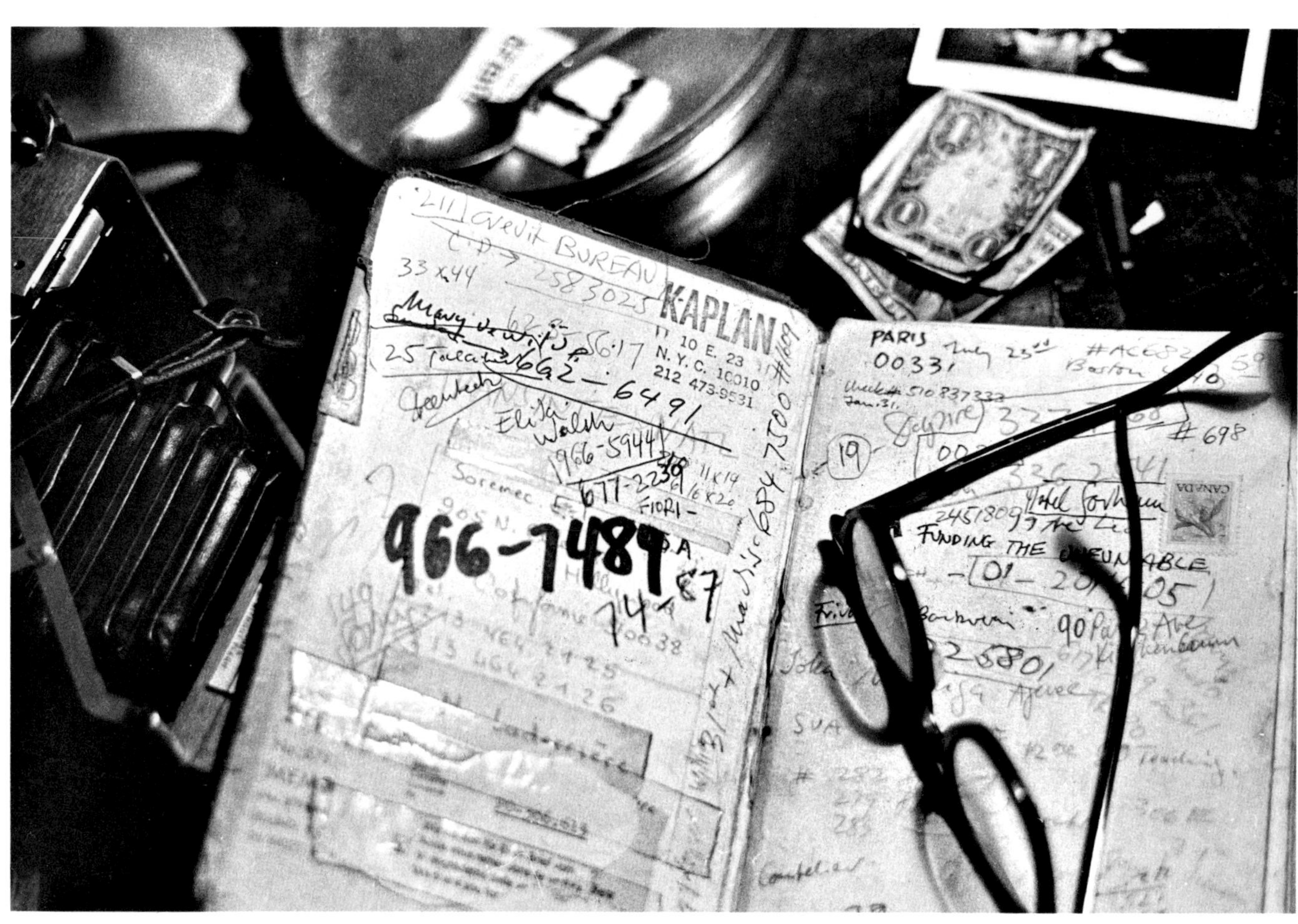

Robert's notebook, NYC, 1981   2nd Avenue thrift shop, NYC, 1981

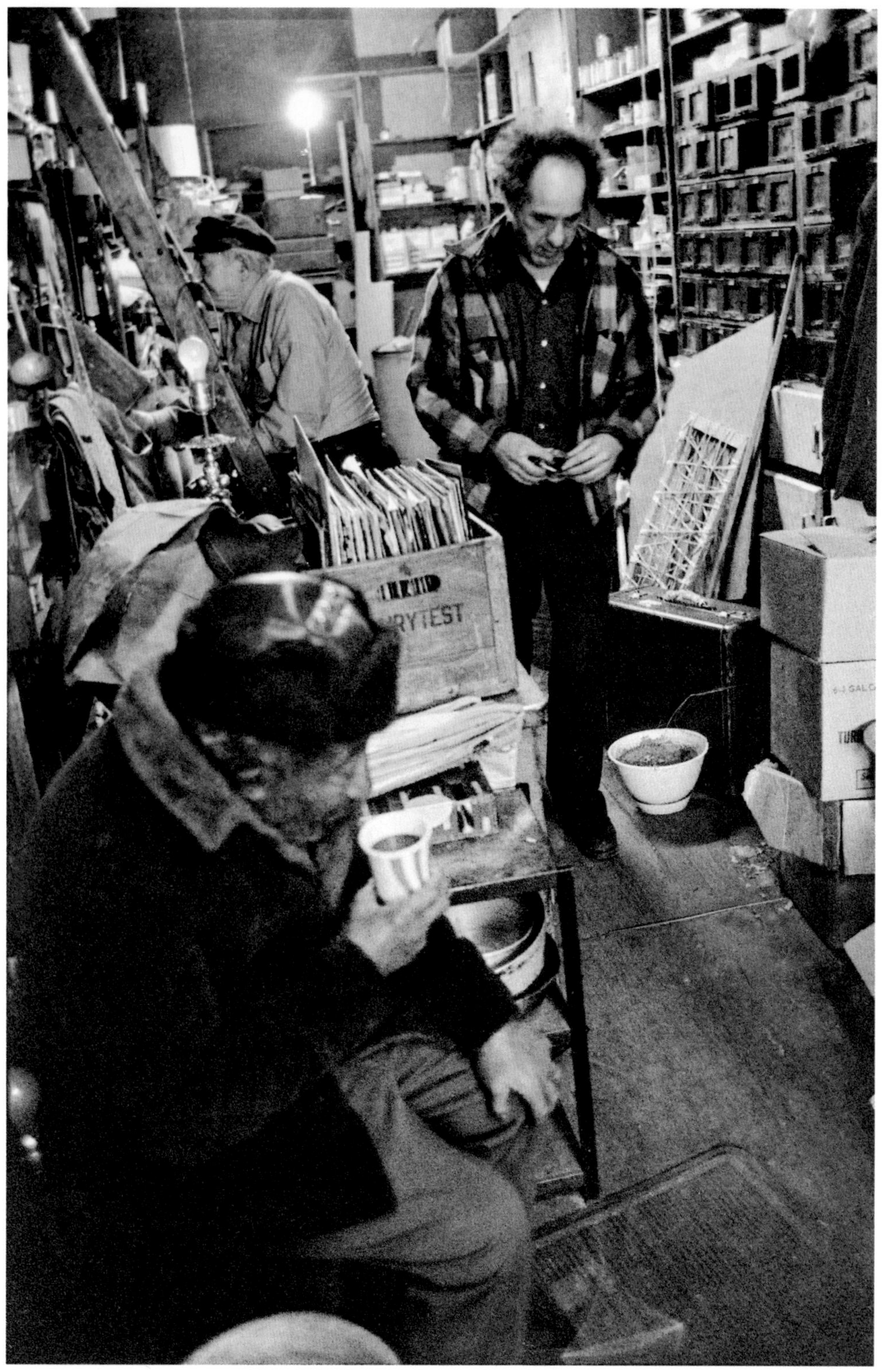

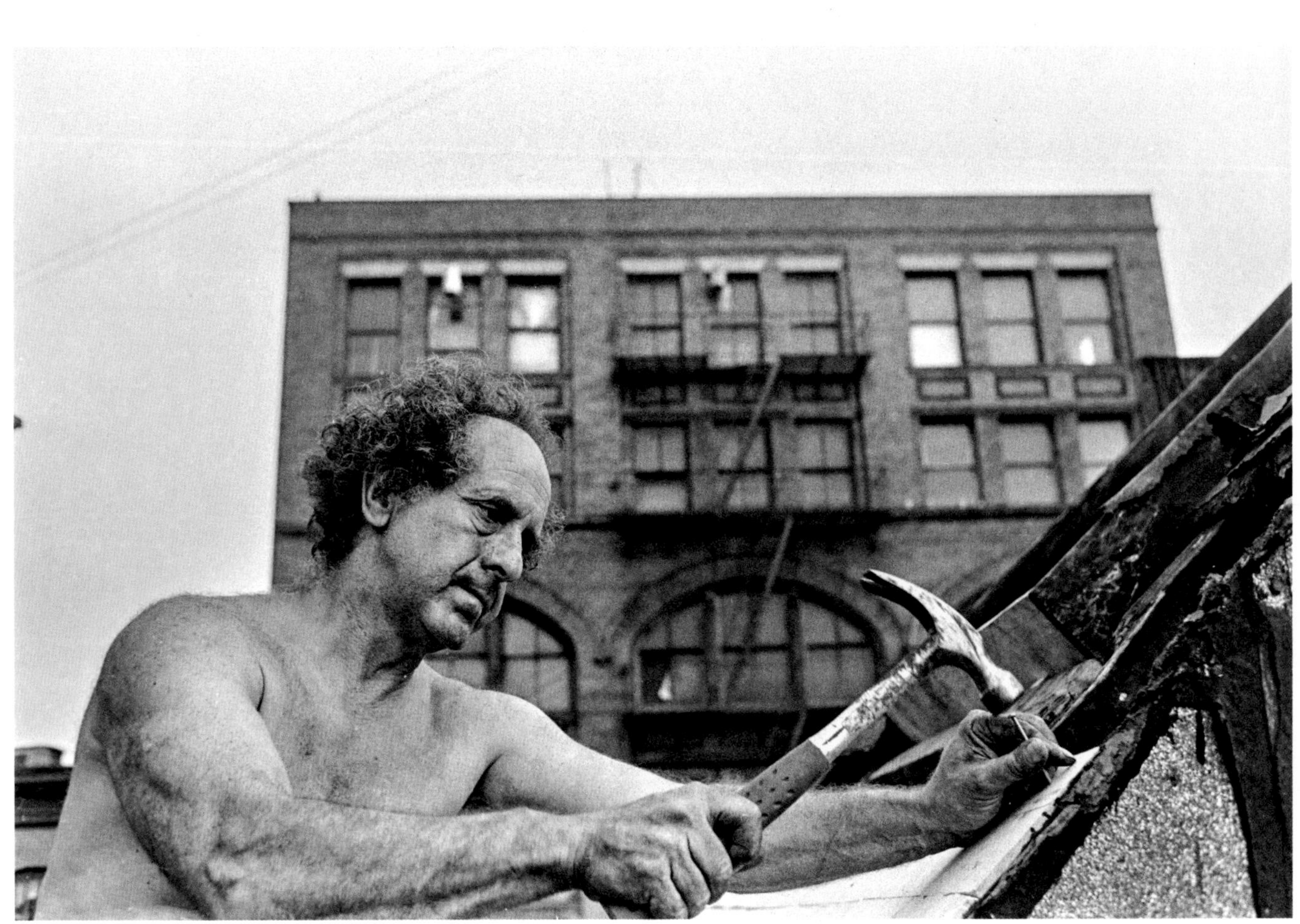

Roof repair, 7 Bleecker Street, NYC, 1981

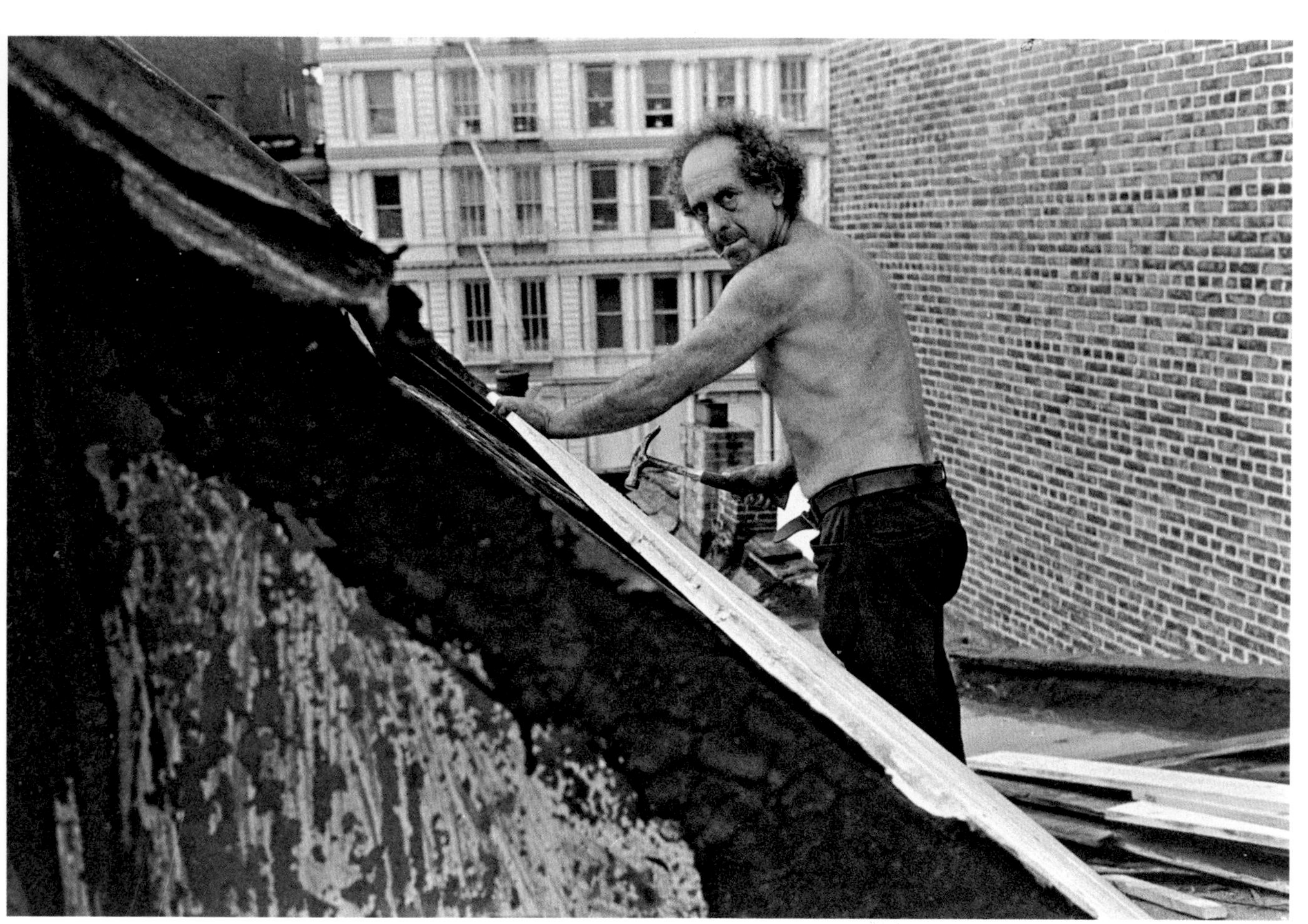

Getting to know Robert, 7 Bleecker Street, NYC, 1981

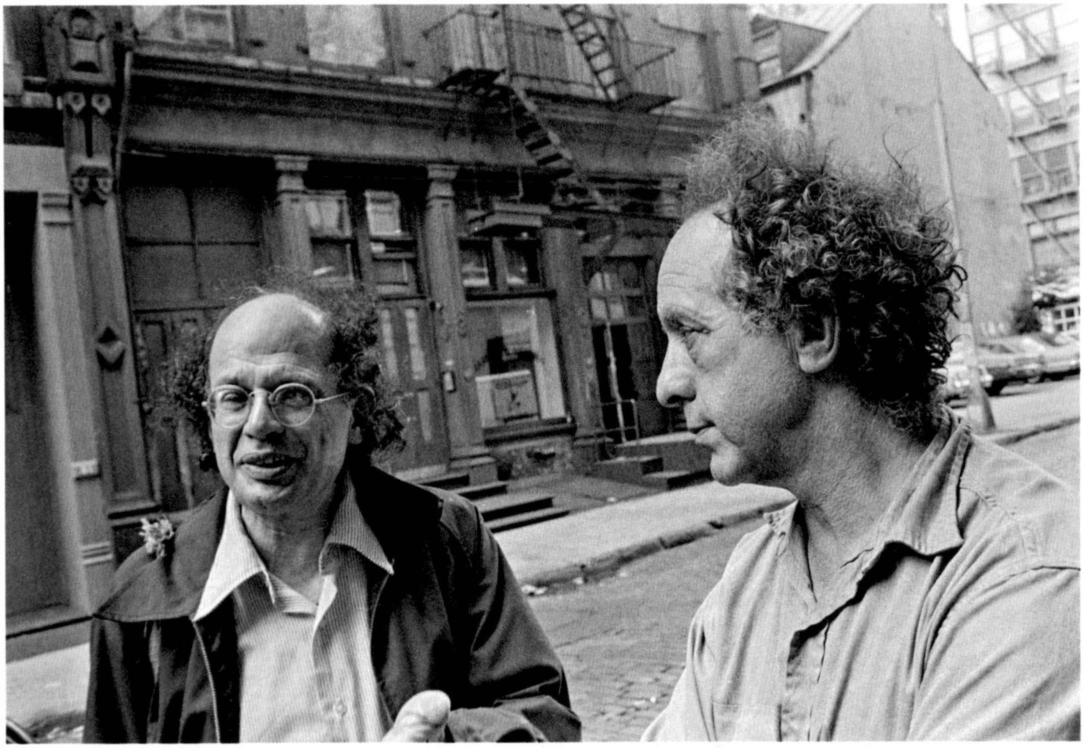

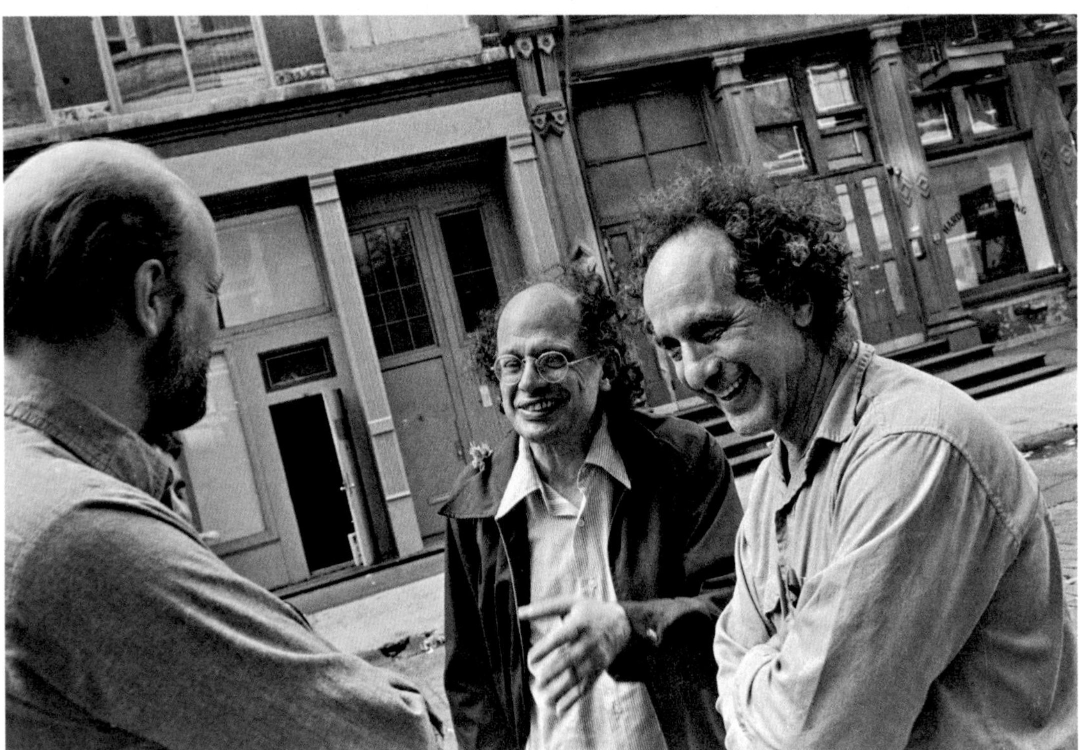

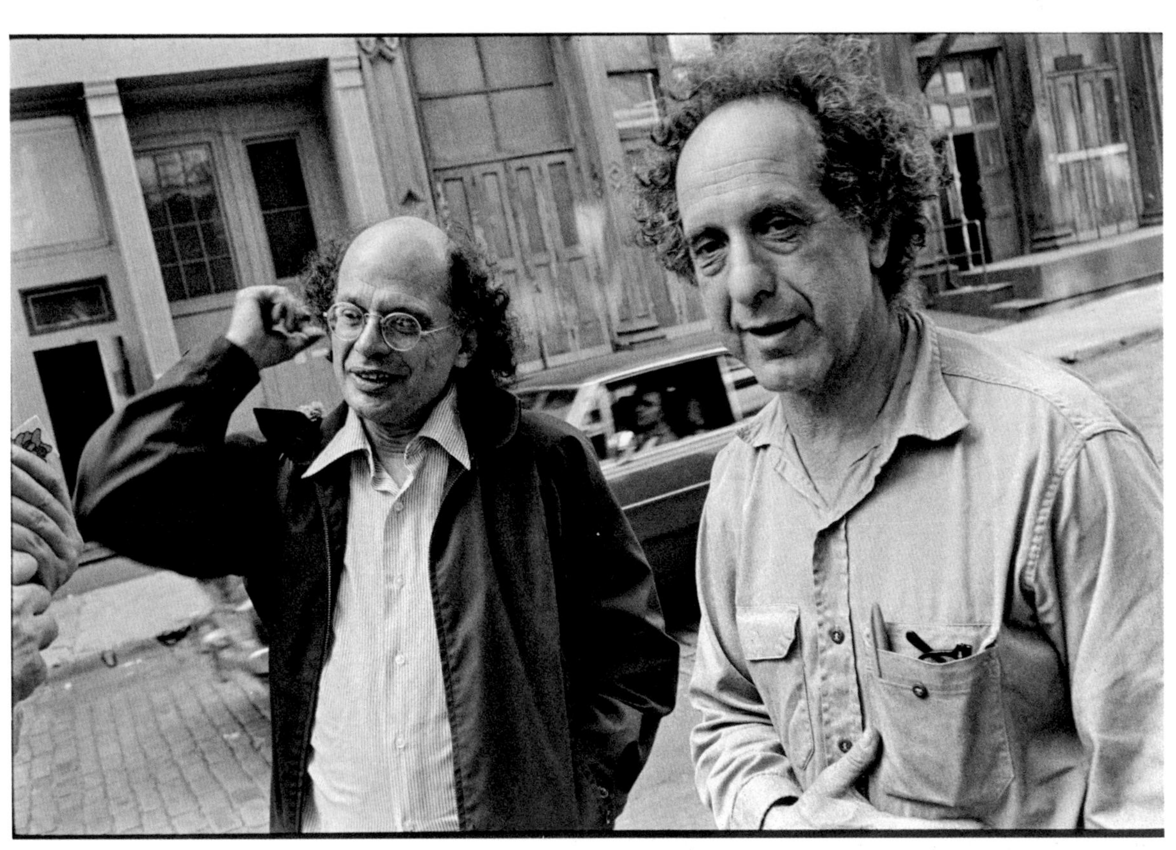

Rudy Wurlitzer, Allen Ginsberg and Robert following
the screening of *Energy and How to Get It*, NYC, 1981

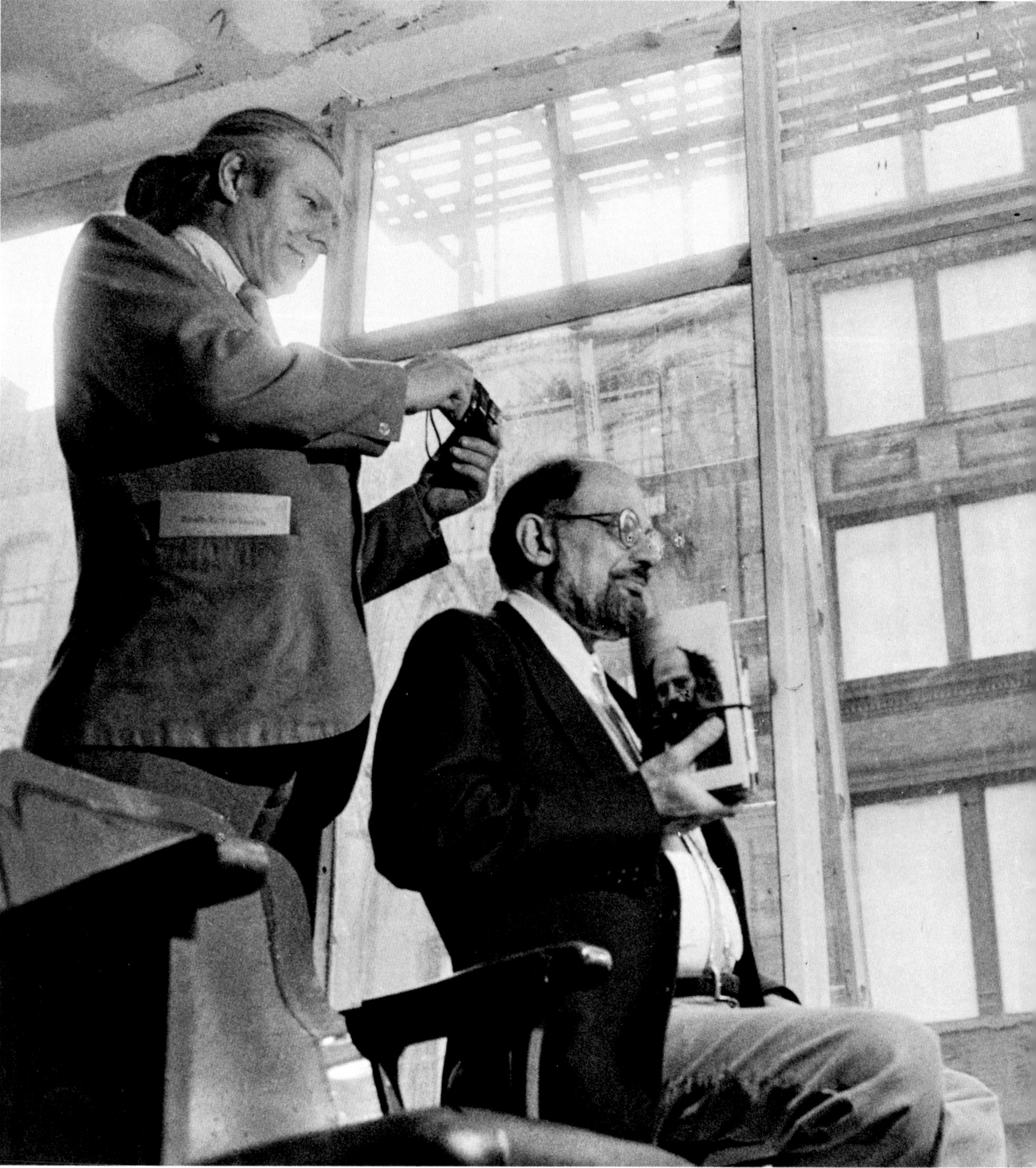

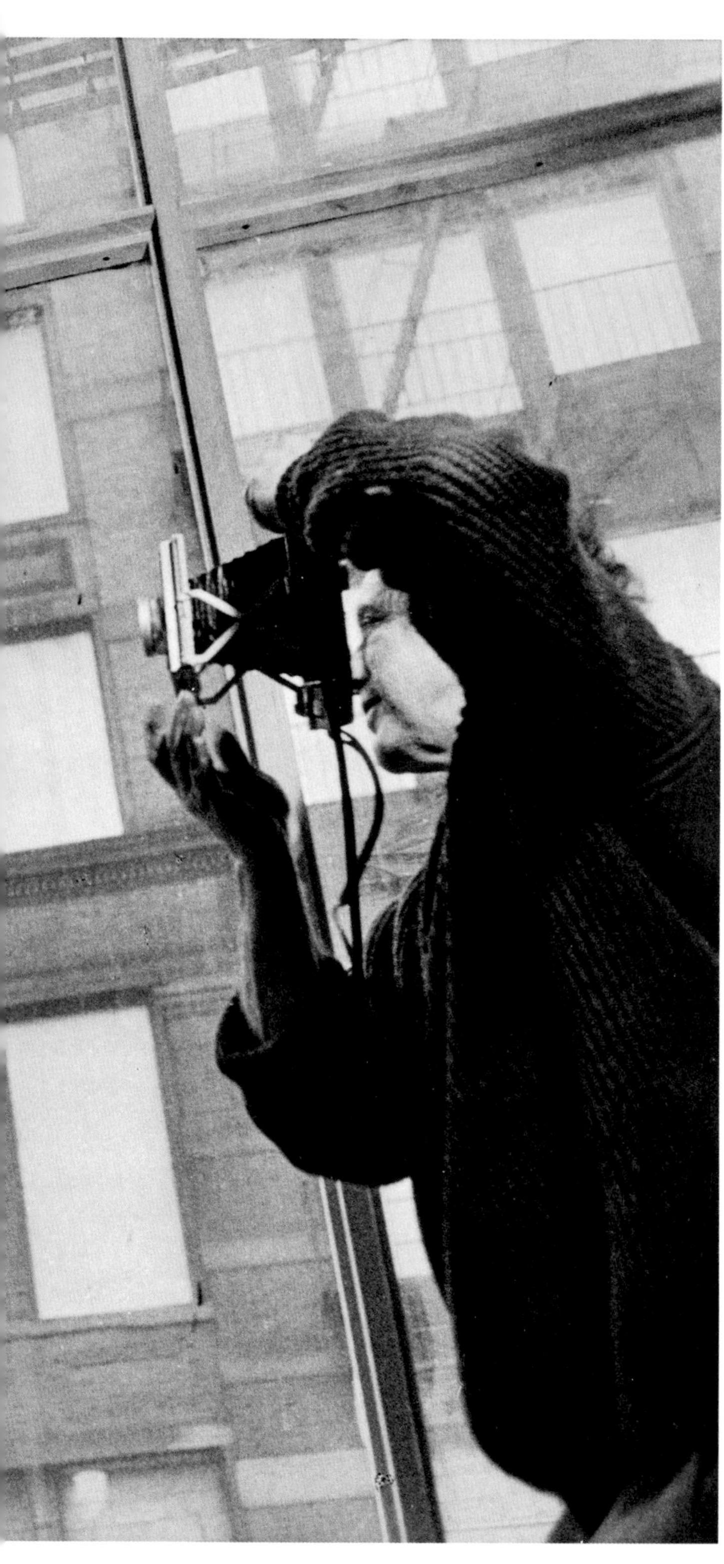

Robert making a portrait for Allen Ginsberg's
Collected Poems, 7 Bleecker Street, NYC, 1984

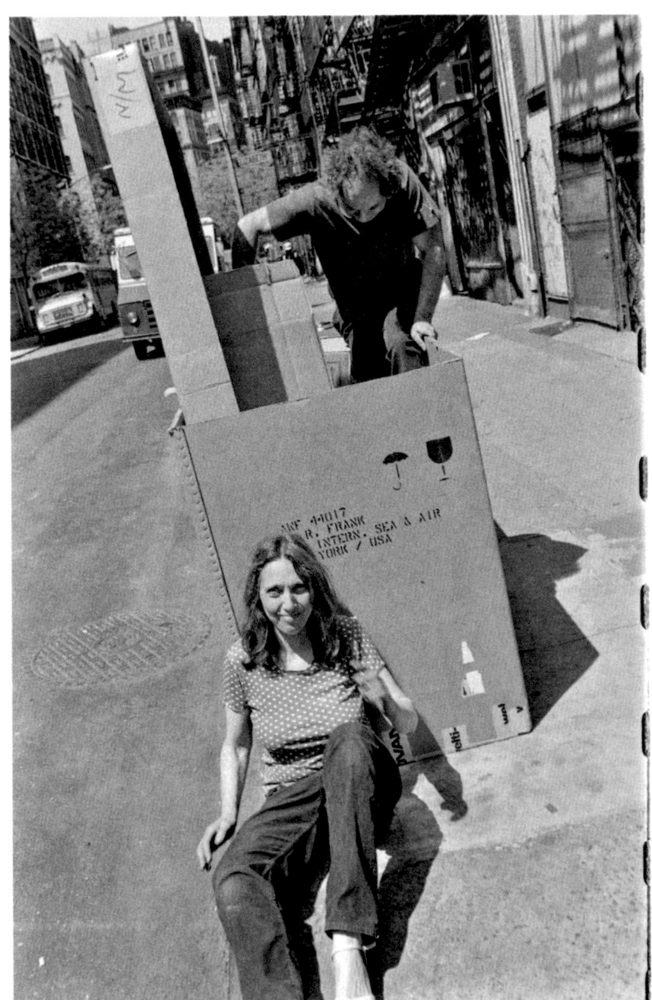
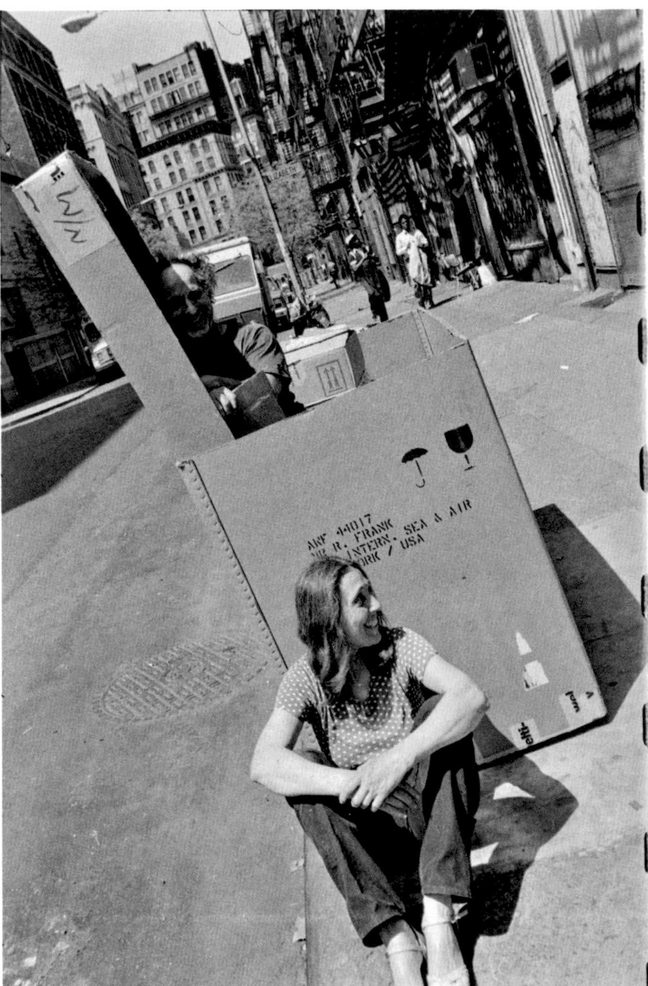

Robert and June in front of 7 Bleecker Street, NYC, 1982

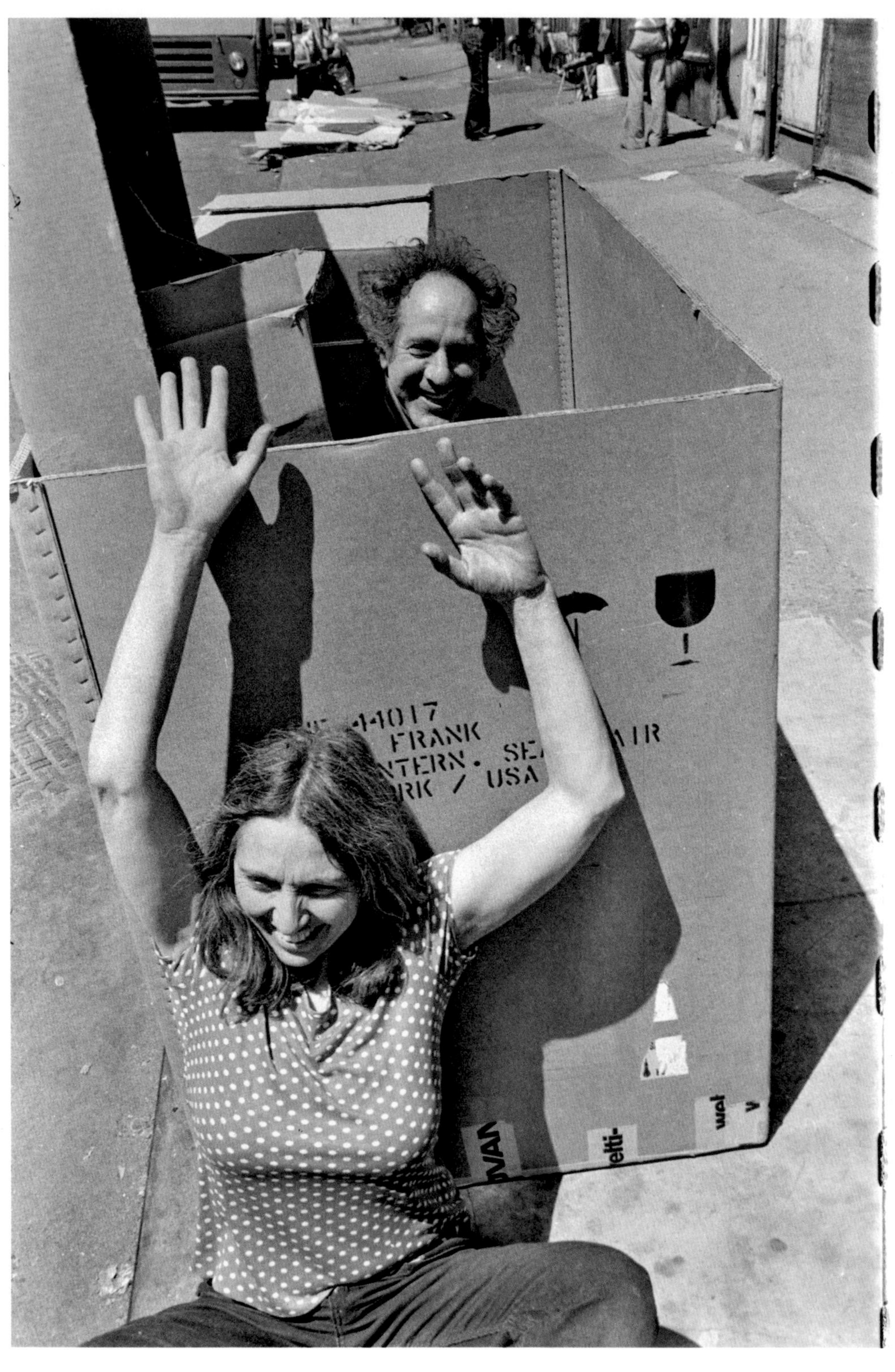

FRANK
NTERN.
RK / USA
14017
SE
IR
VAN
etti
wel
v

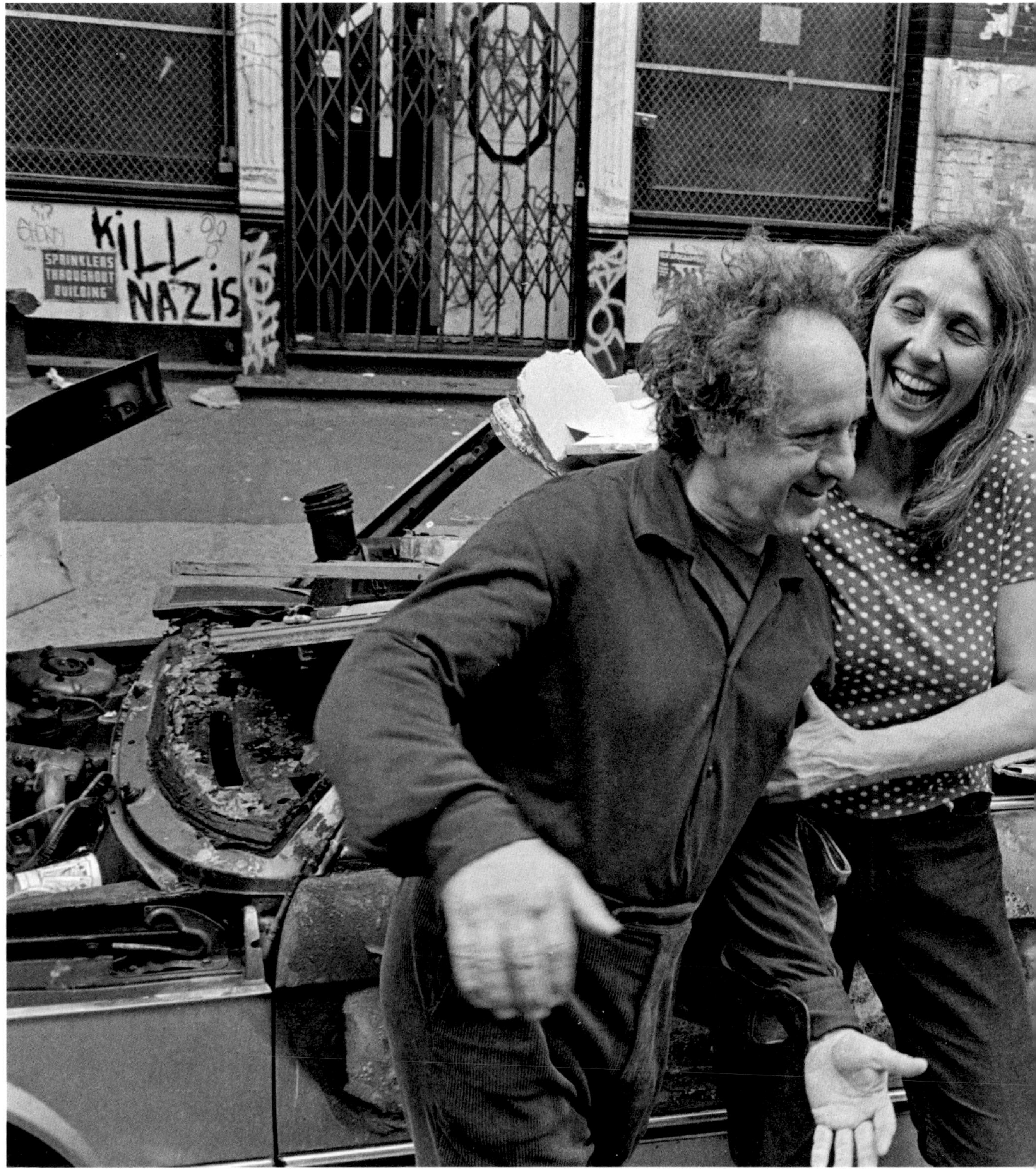

KILL
NAZIS
SPRINKLERS
THROUGHOUT
BUILDING

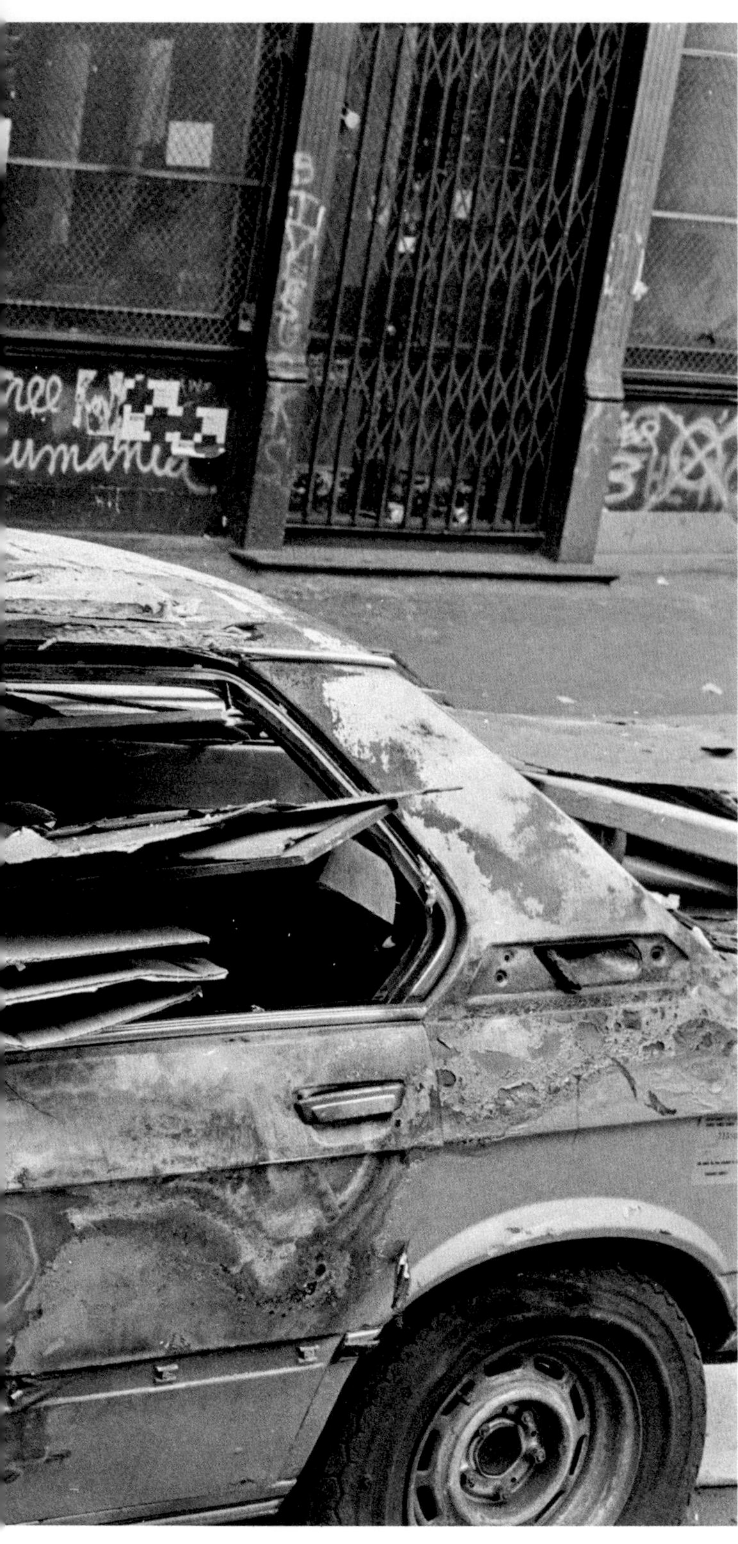

Robert and June in front of 10 Bleecker Street, NYC, 1982

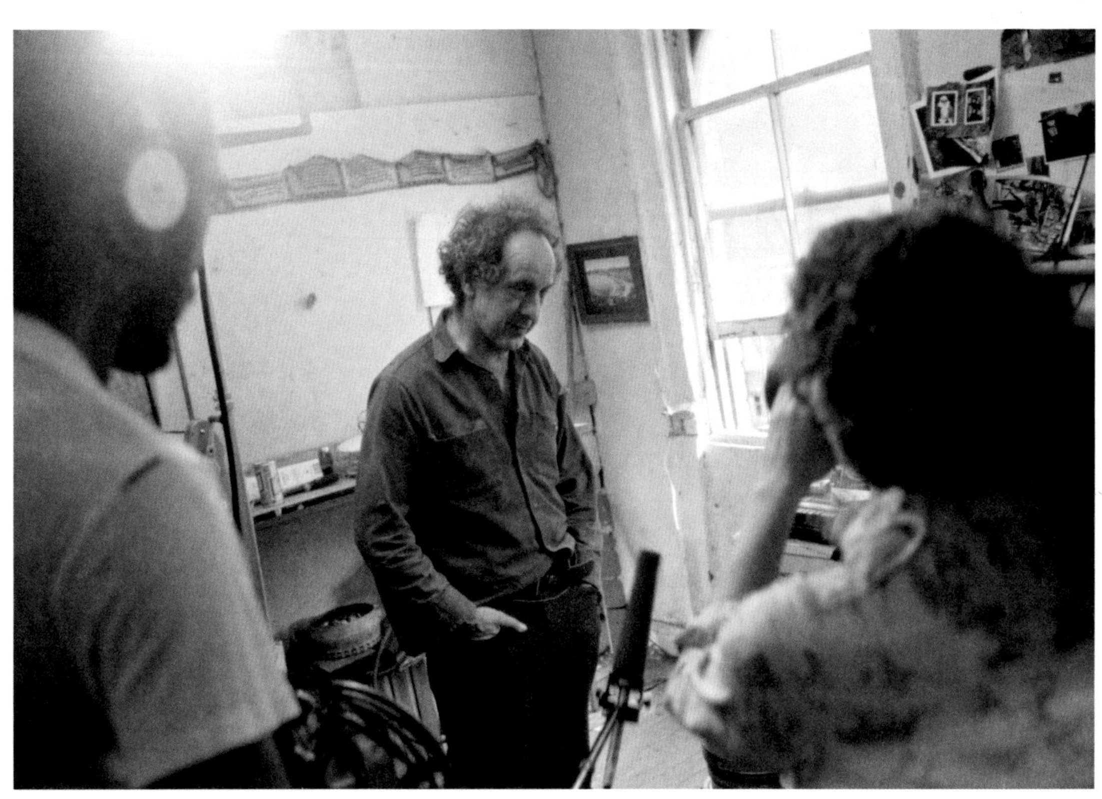

Robert being interviewed,
7 Bleecker Street, NYC, 1982

Robert unpacking family heirlooms sent
from Zurich to 7 Bleecker Street, NYC, 1982

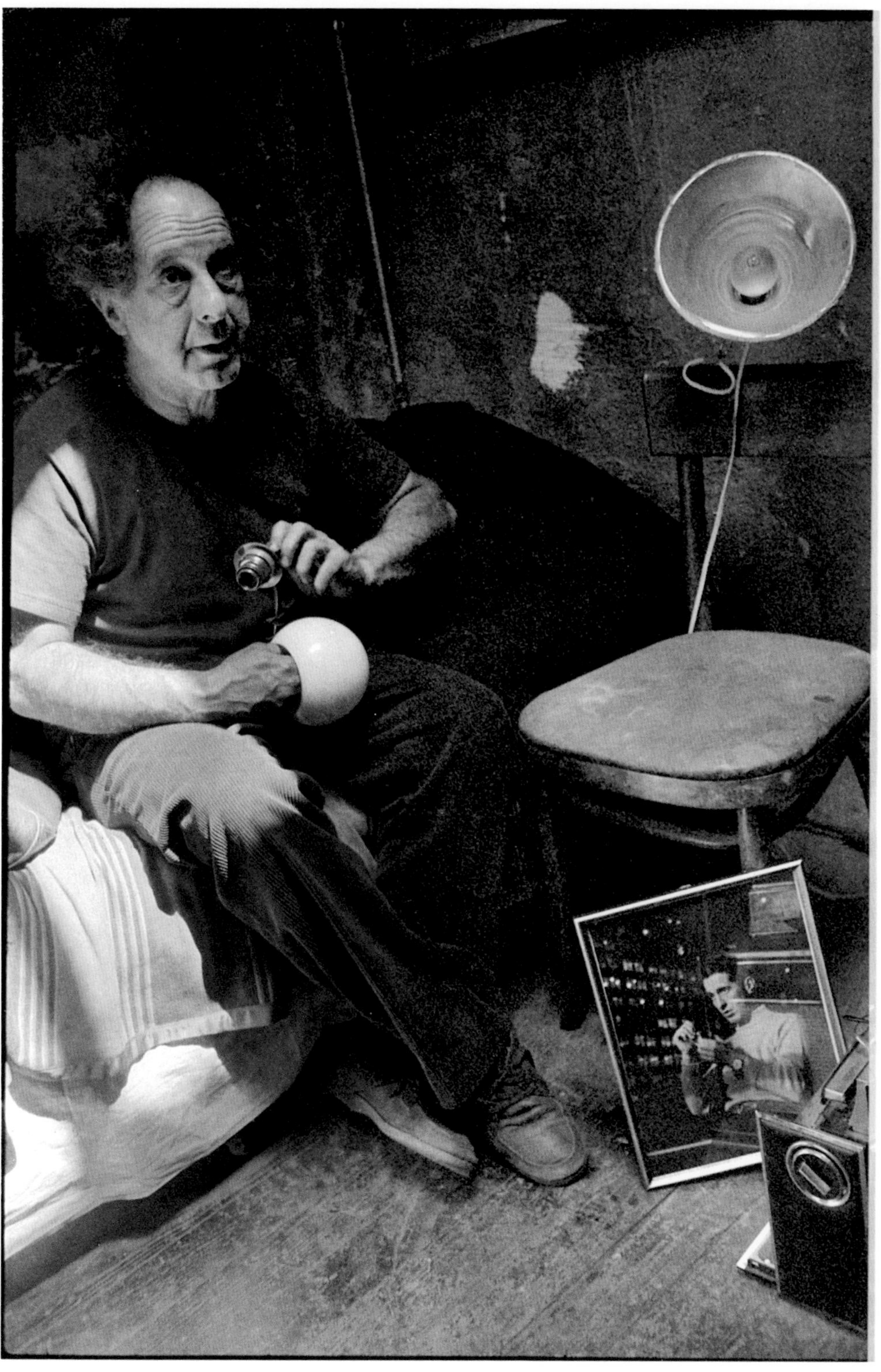

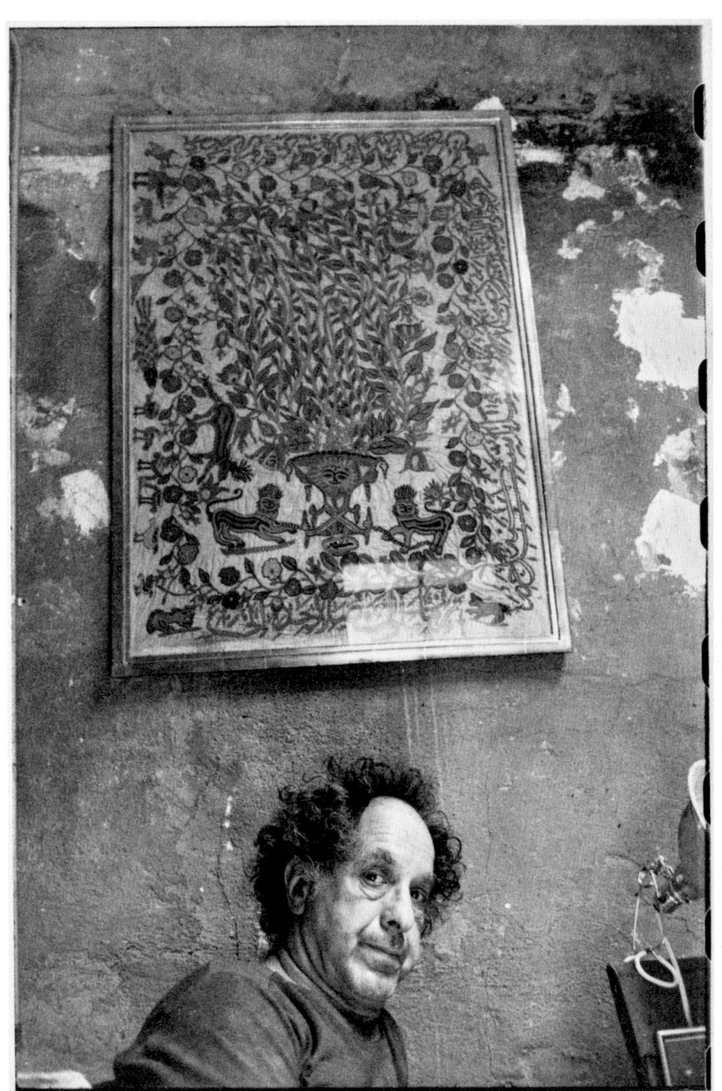
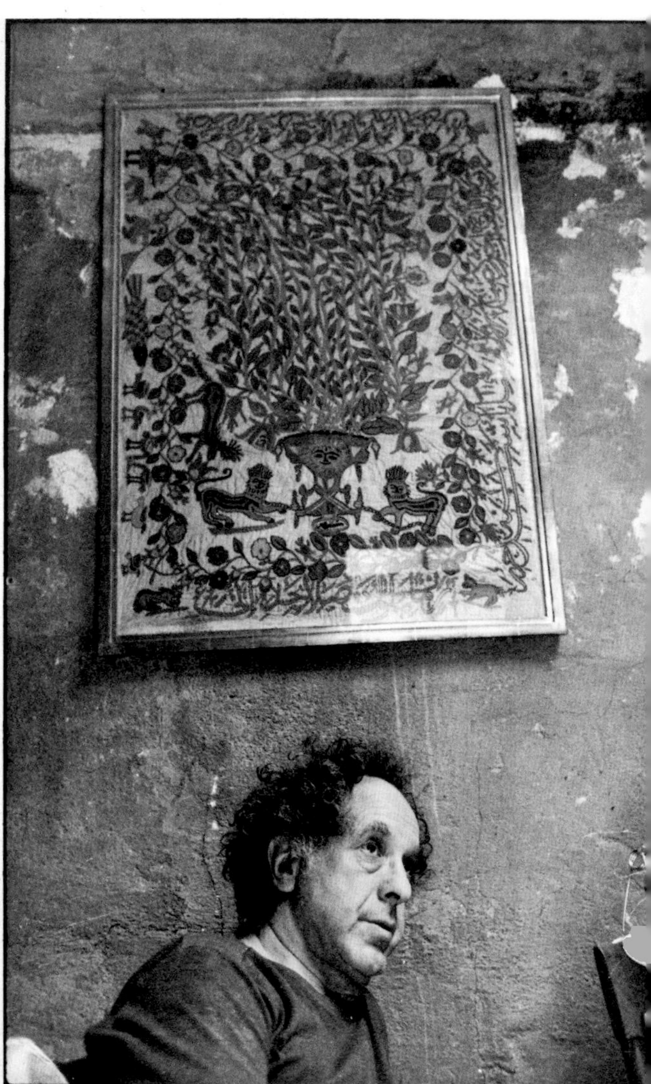

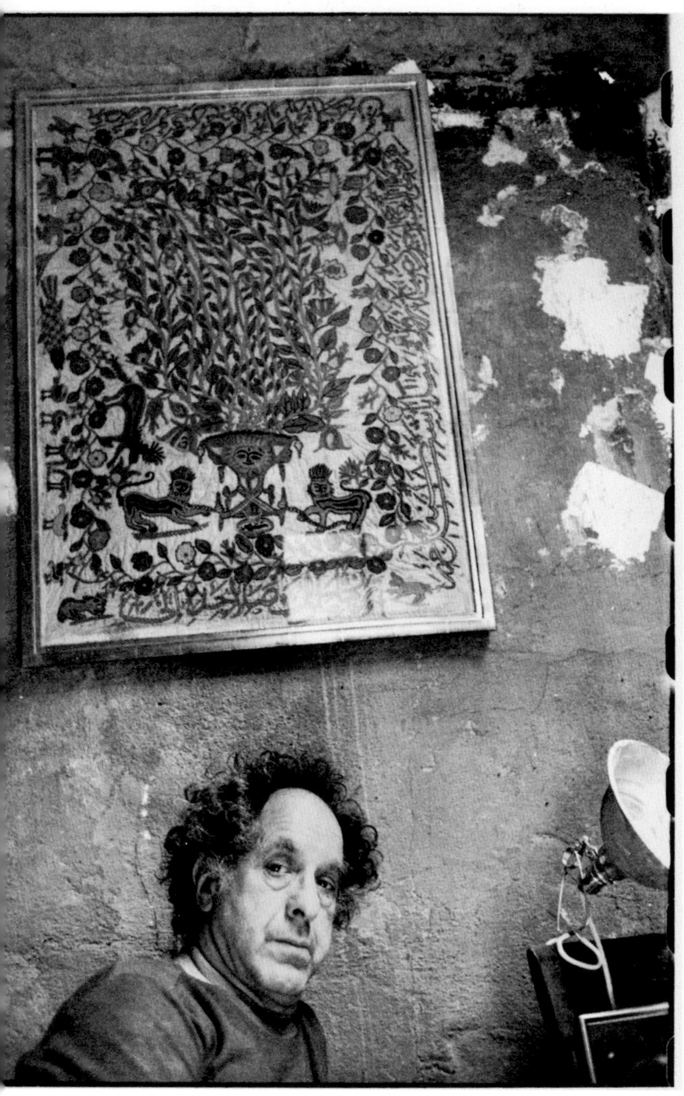

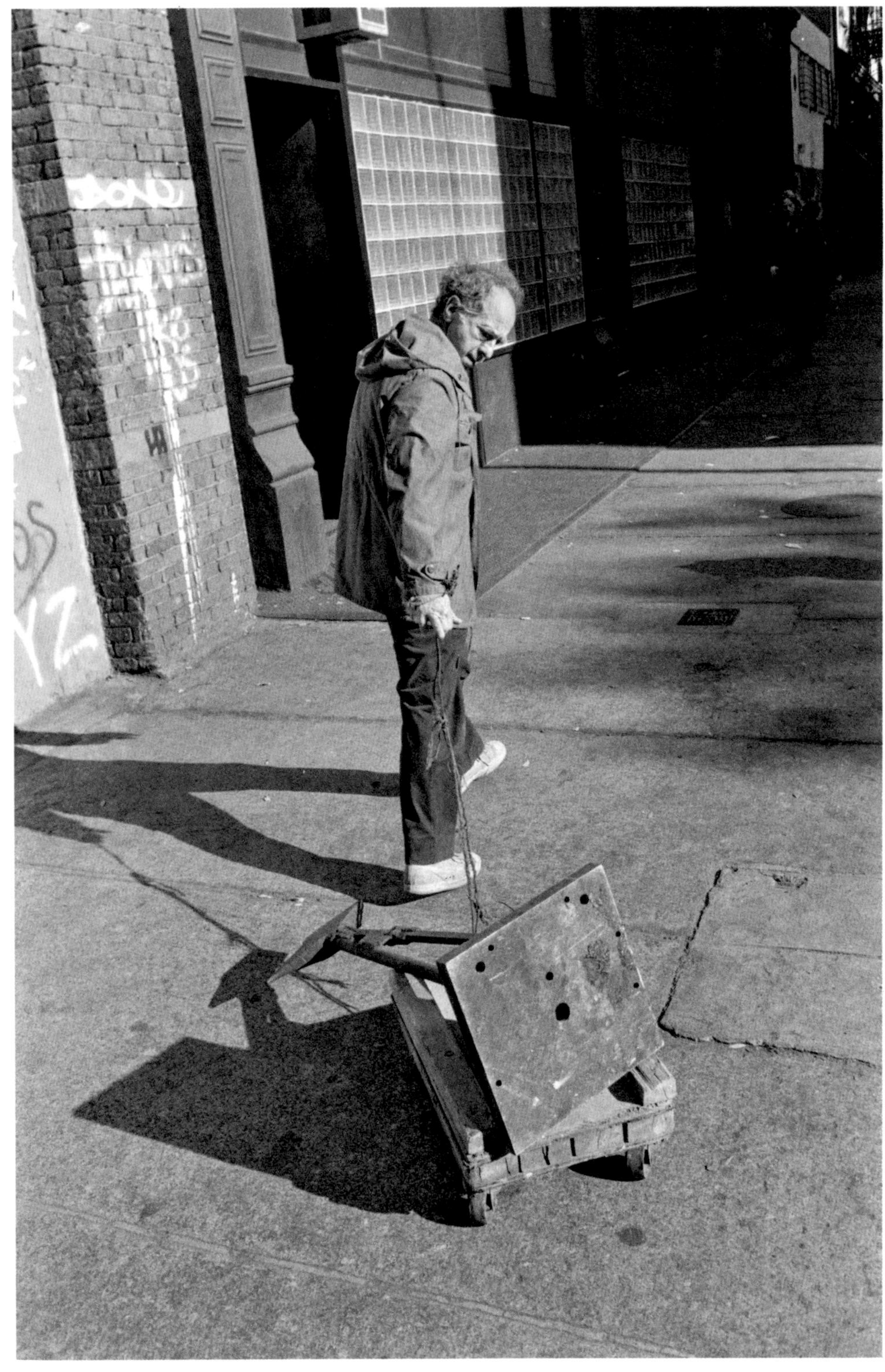

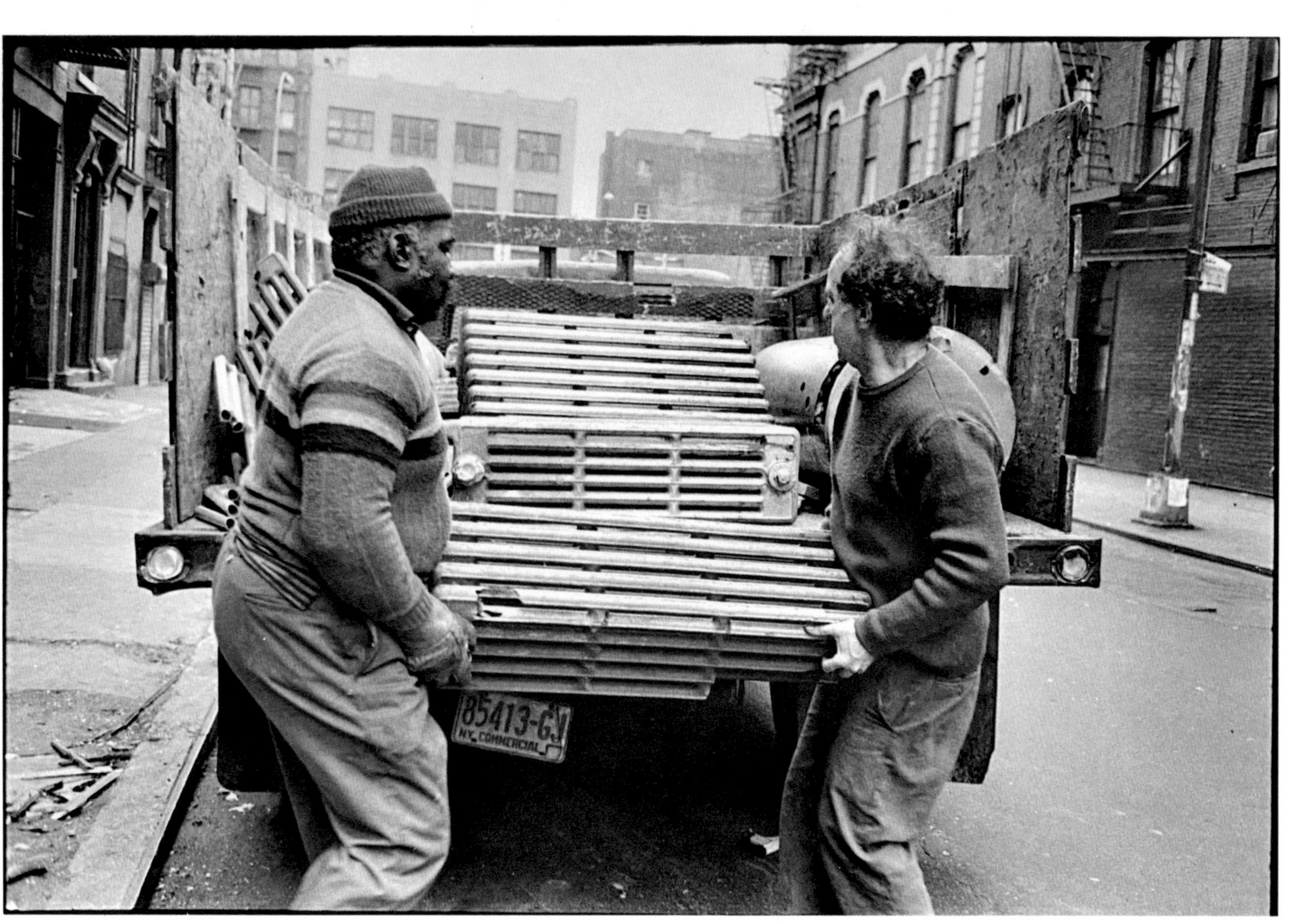

Coming Home with Found Object (Anvil),
Bleecker Street, NYC, 1988

Robert helps the salvage man, 7 Bleecker Street near Bowery, 1982

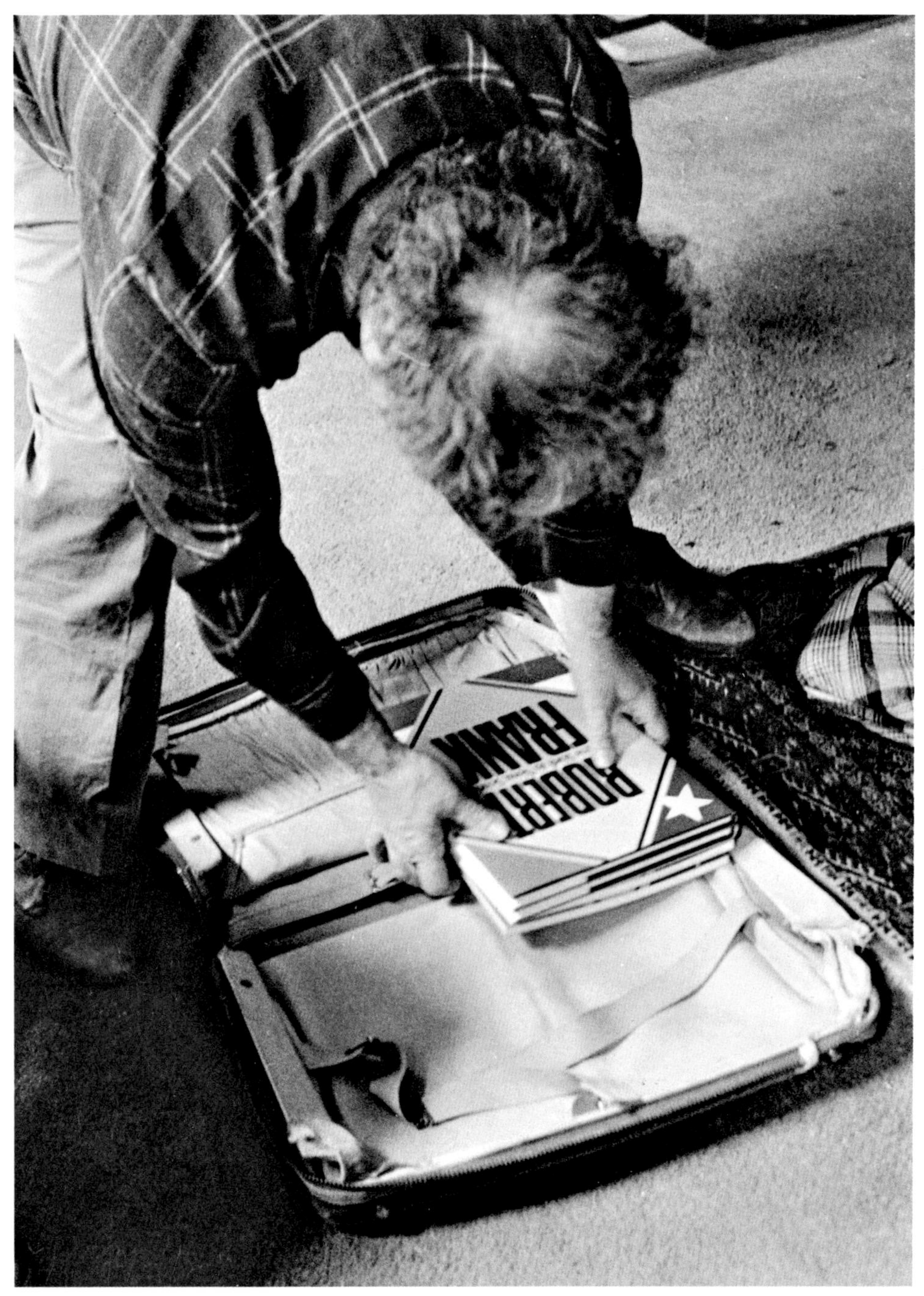

New York to Nova Scotia catalogues from his Houston exhibition

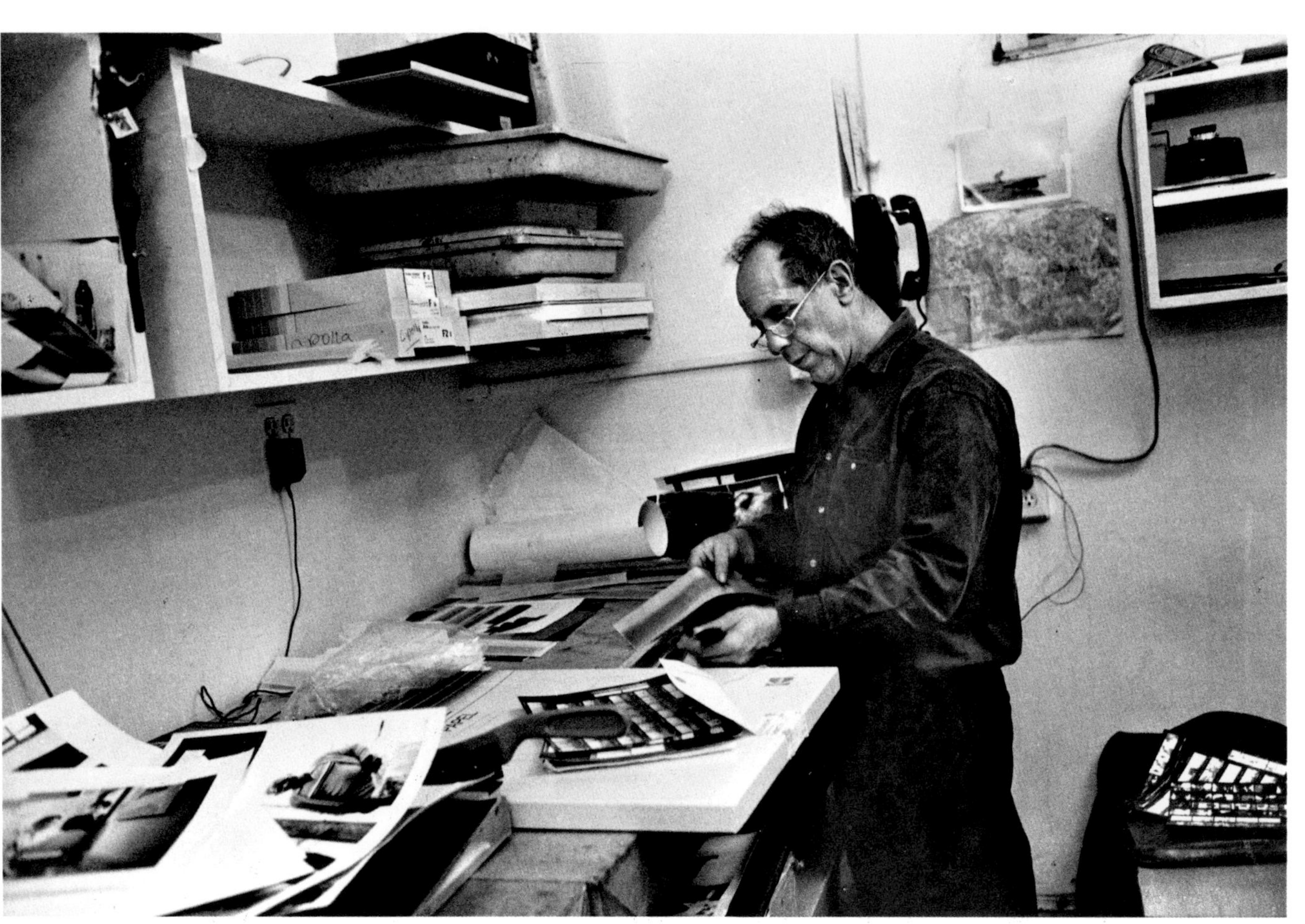

My darkroom at 101 Crosby Street, NYC, 1987

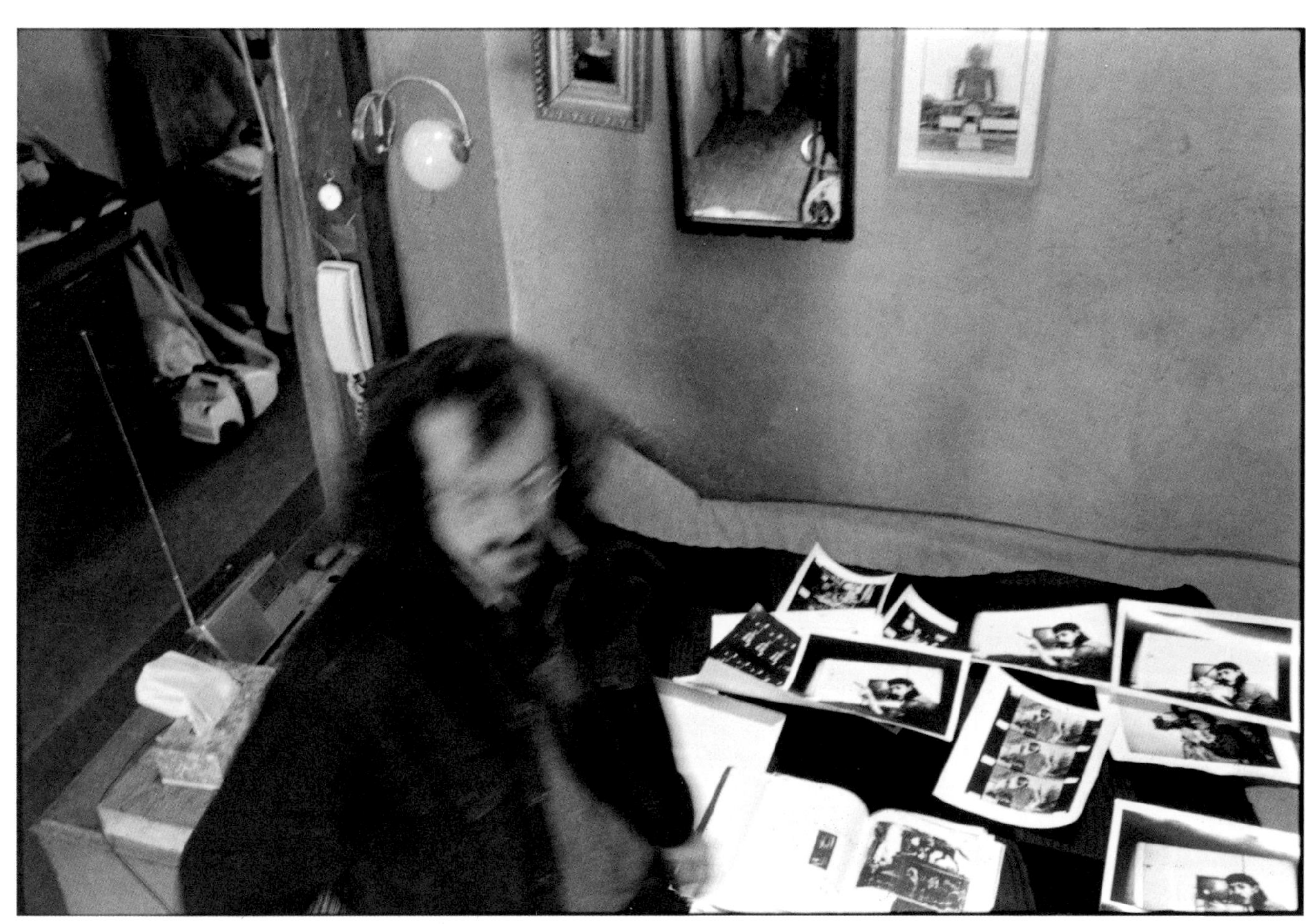

Selecting prints for the Scalo edition of *The Lines of My Hand*, NYC, 1988

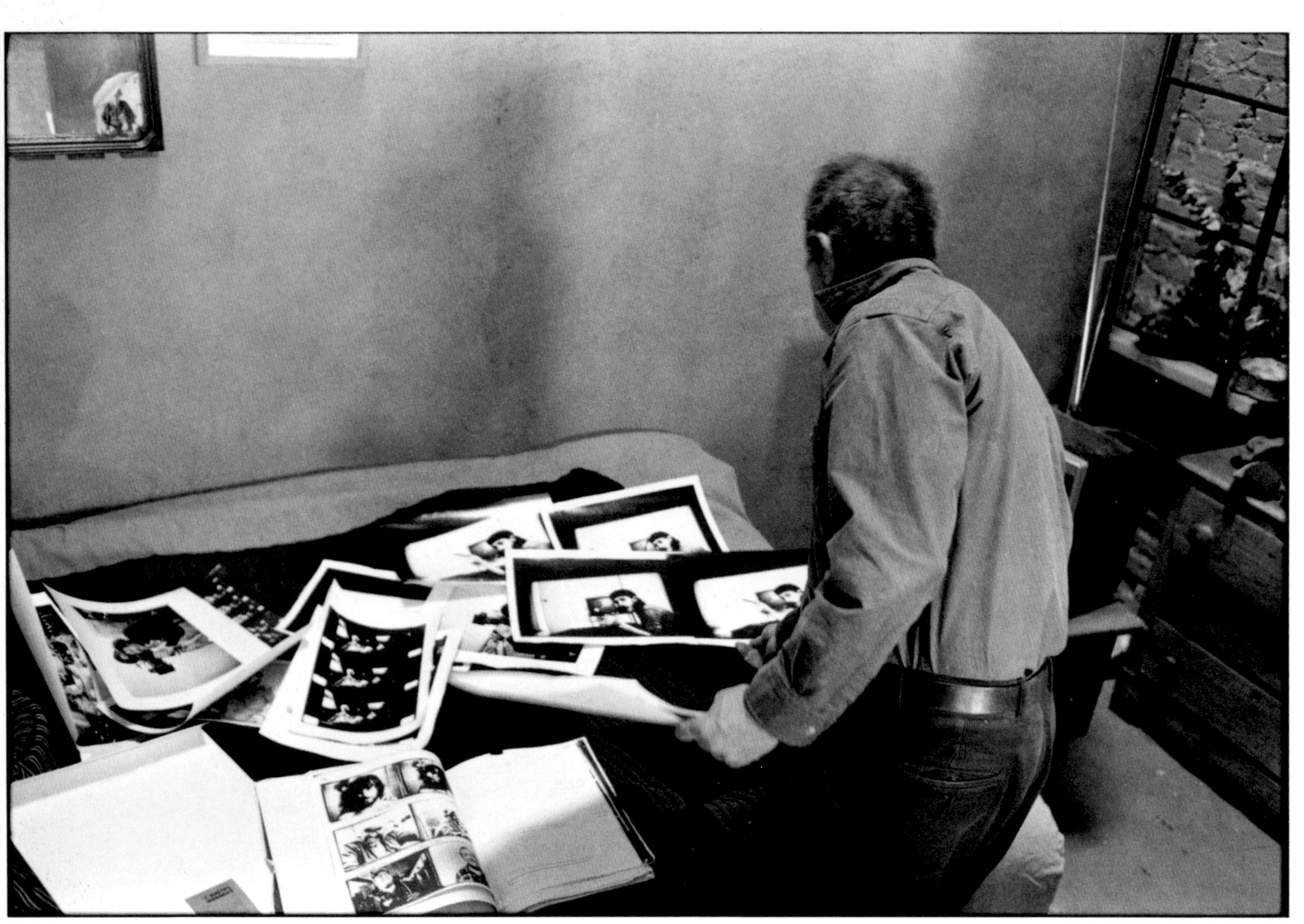

Inverness woman missing

An Inverness woman was placed on the RCMP's missing persons list Tuesday morning following her disappearance at the Broad Cove concert on July 24.

Tracey Lee Wiswell, 22, was last seen at the concert, and apparently called home from Halifax on Tuesday, July 27.

However, new information has her family worried that she may have been calling from North Sydney and not Halifax. In any event, she hasn't been heard from since.

Wiswell was wearing black and white stretch pants, a t-shirt and black leather jacket when last seen. Her family said it is highly unusual for her to disappear without calling or letting anybody know where she was going.

She was carrying a blue shoulder bag but did not have any spare clothing packed. She was also believed to have just a few dollars on her.

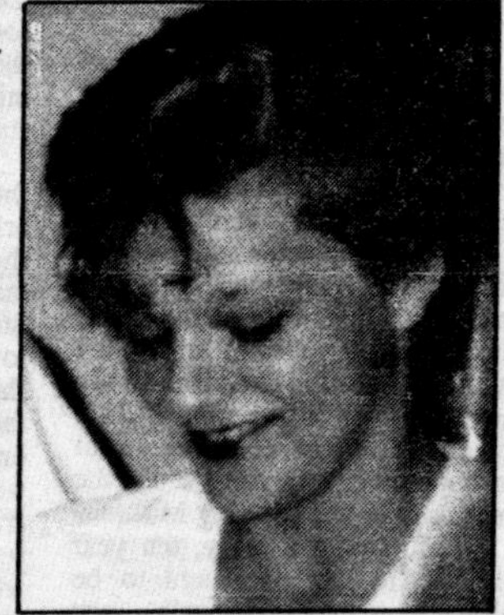

TRACEY WISWELL

Anybody with *any* information on her whereabouts or her intentions before leaving is asked to call her mother, Florence, at 258-3615, or the Inverness detachment of the RCMP, 258-2213.

Hello Brian

l cannot give you further info but it would be advisable for you to get on this case now. Can you imagine yourself on a horse riding across Kelley,s Mountainhaving rescued Tracey from theIndians. l am making a Film called "William Tell" so far only the Apple is cast as the son.l chop some wood & we are thinking of having the house jacked up for Home Improvements l wish you well- find her....

Hello again from Robert.

IN MABOU

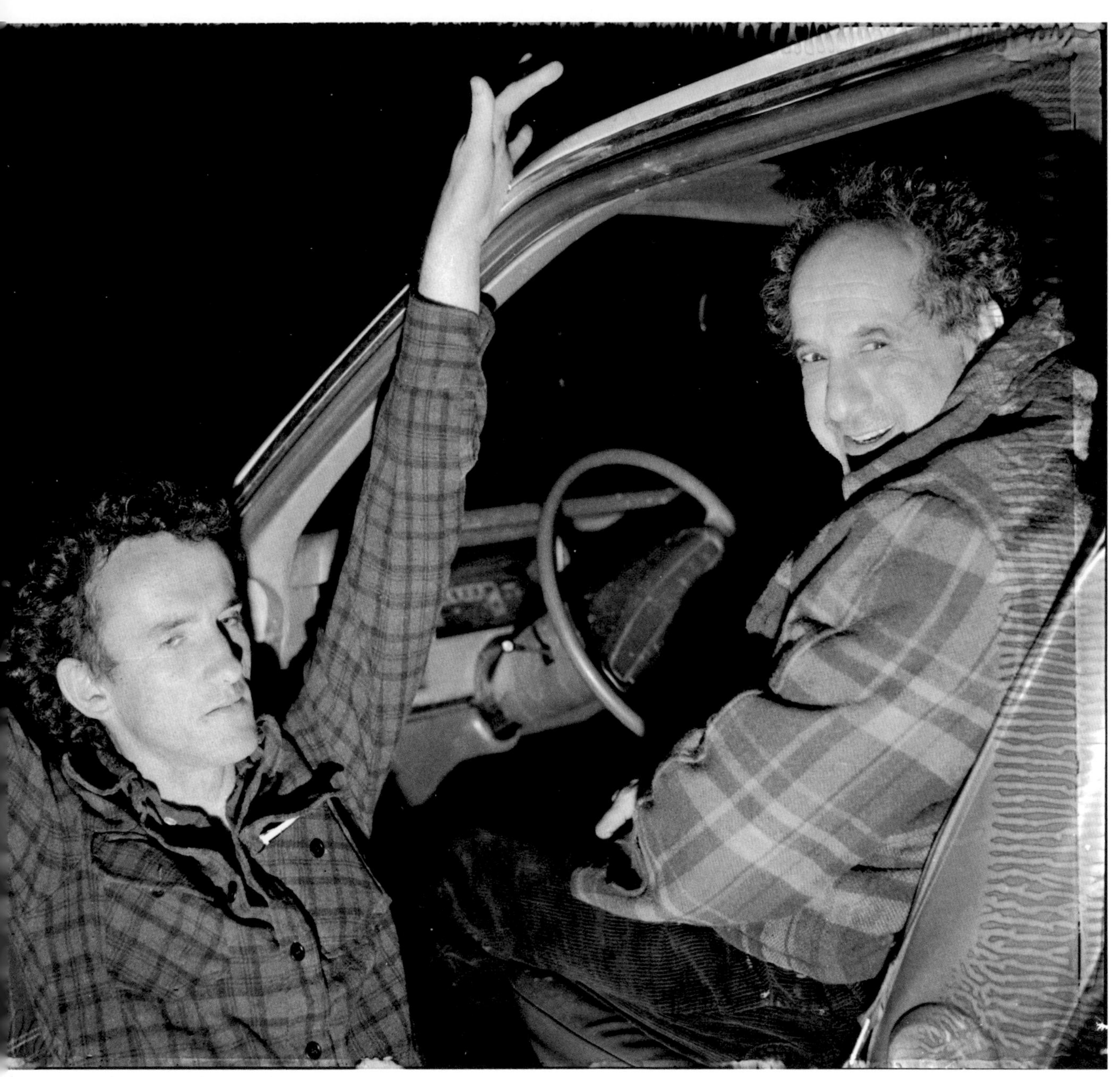

Reg Rankin and R.F., Mabou Mines, 1983

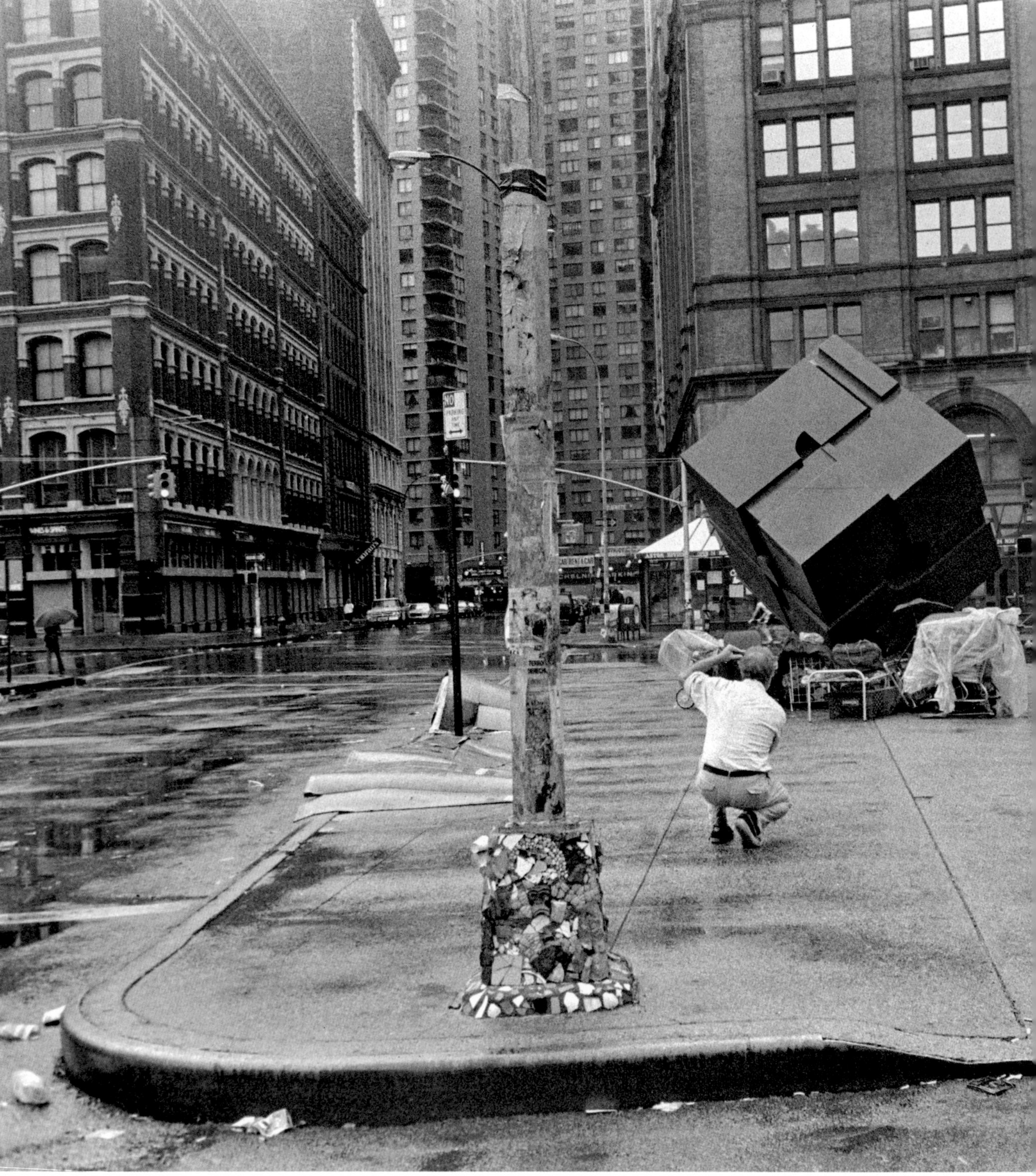

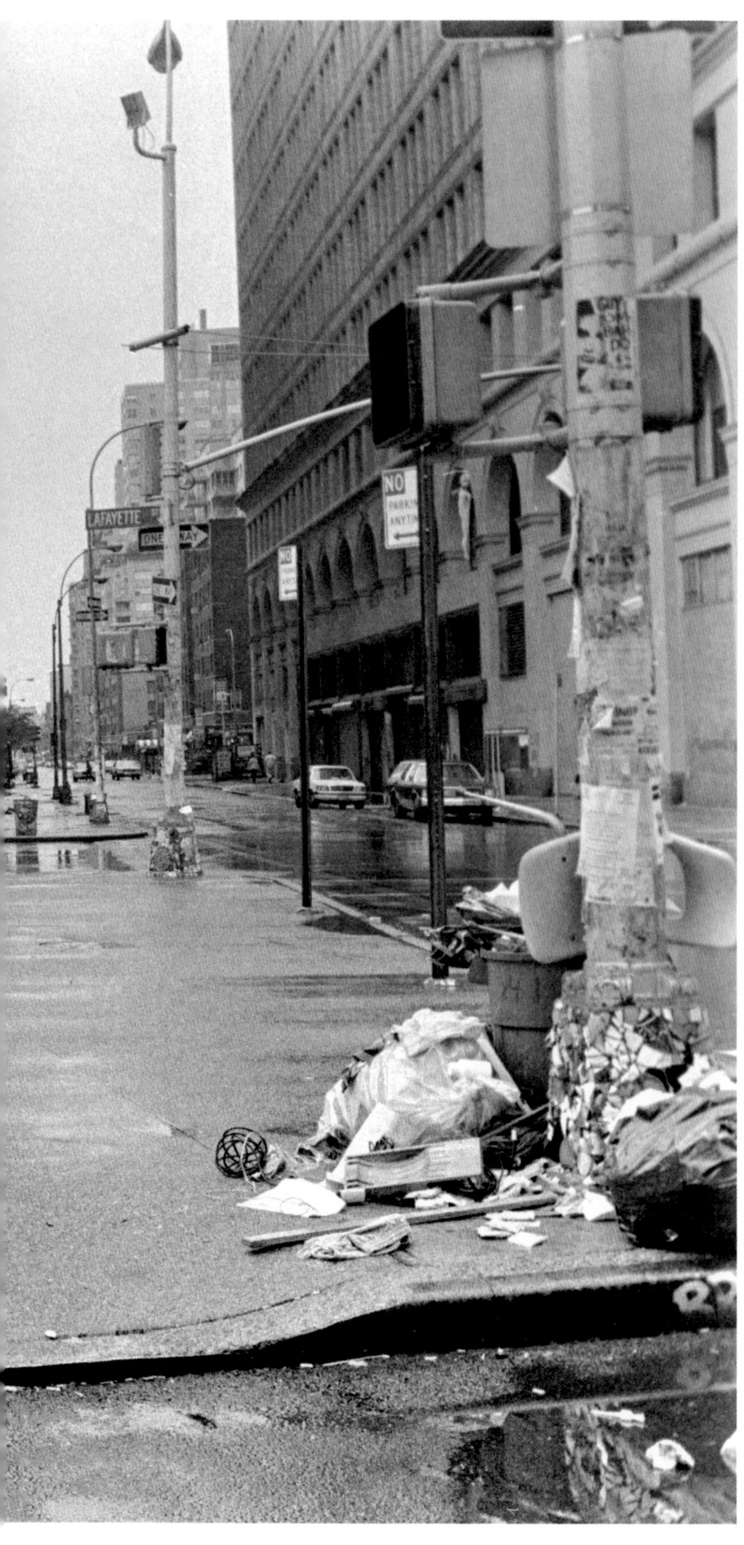

Sunday morning at Astor Place, NYC, June 1992

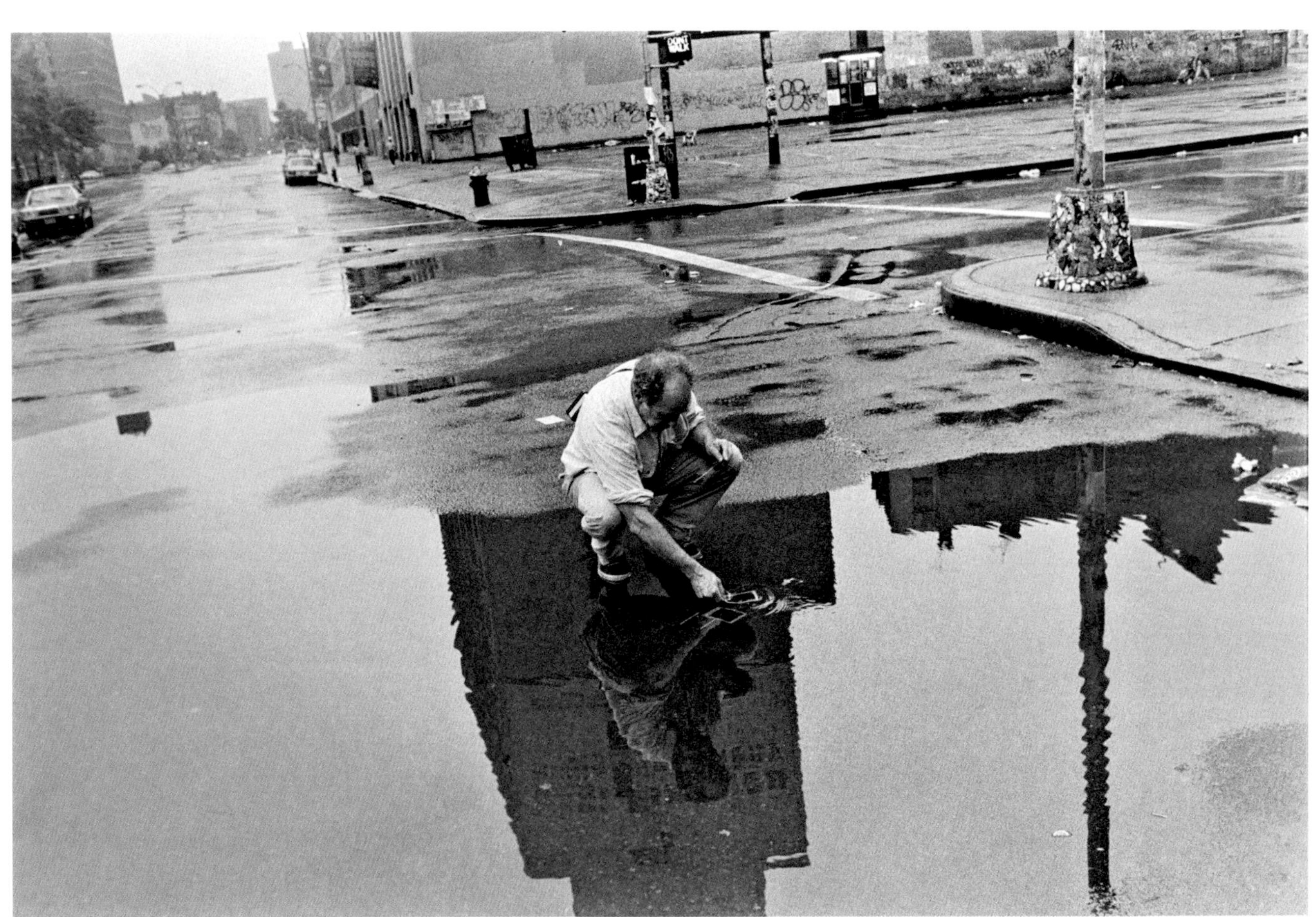

Robert processing Polaroid negatives in fresh
rain water at Astor Place, NYC, June 1992

Robert's photograph

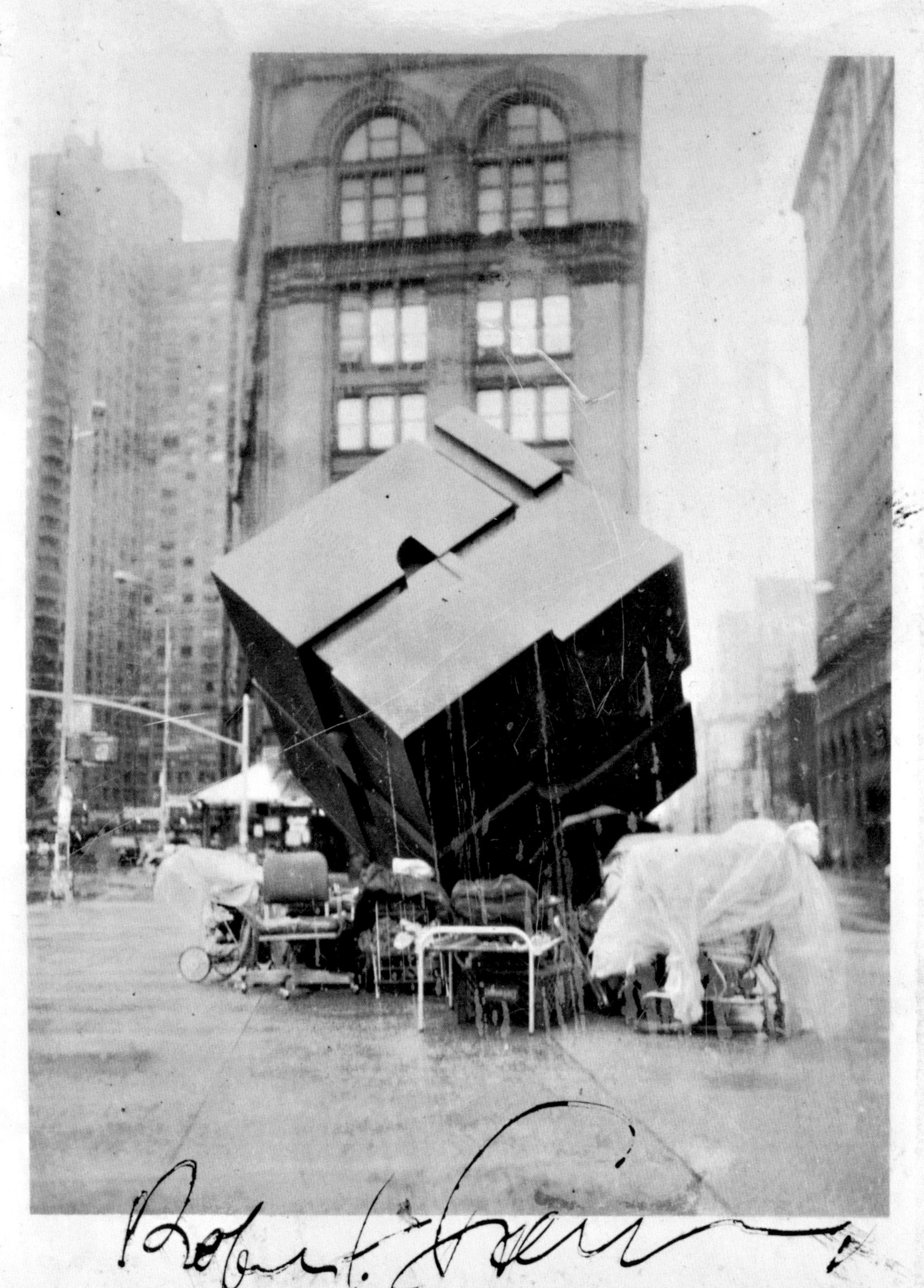

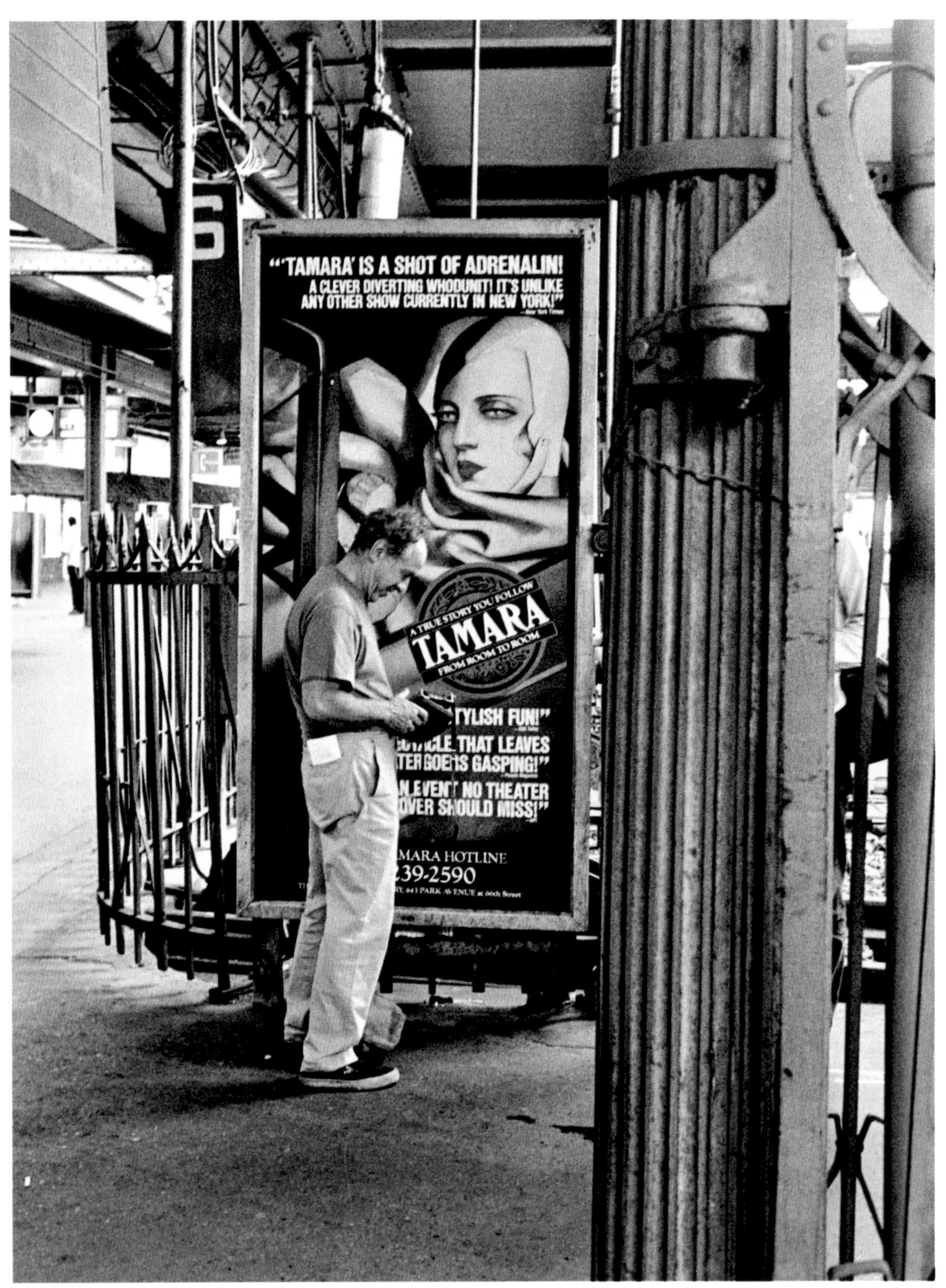

Robert making a Polaroid test for his Aspesi
commission, Hoboken station, New Jersey, 1988

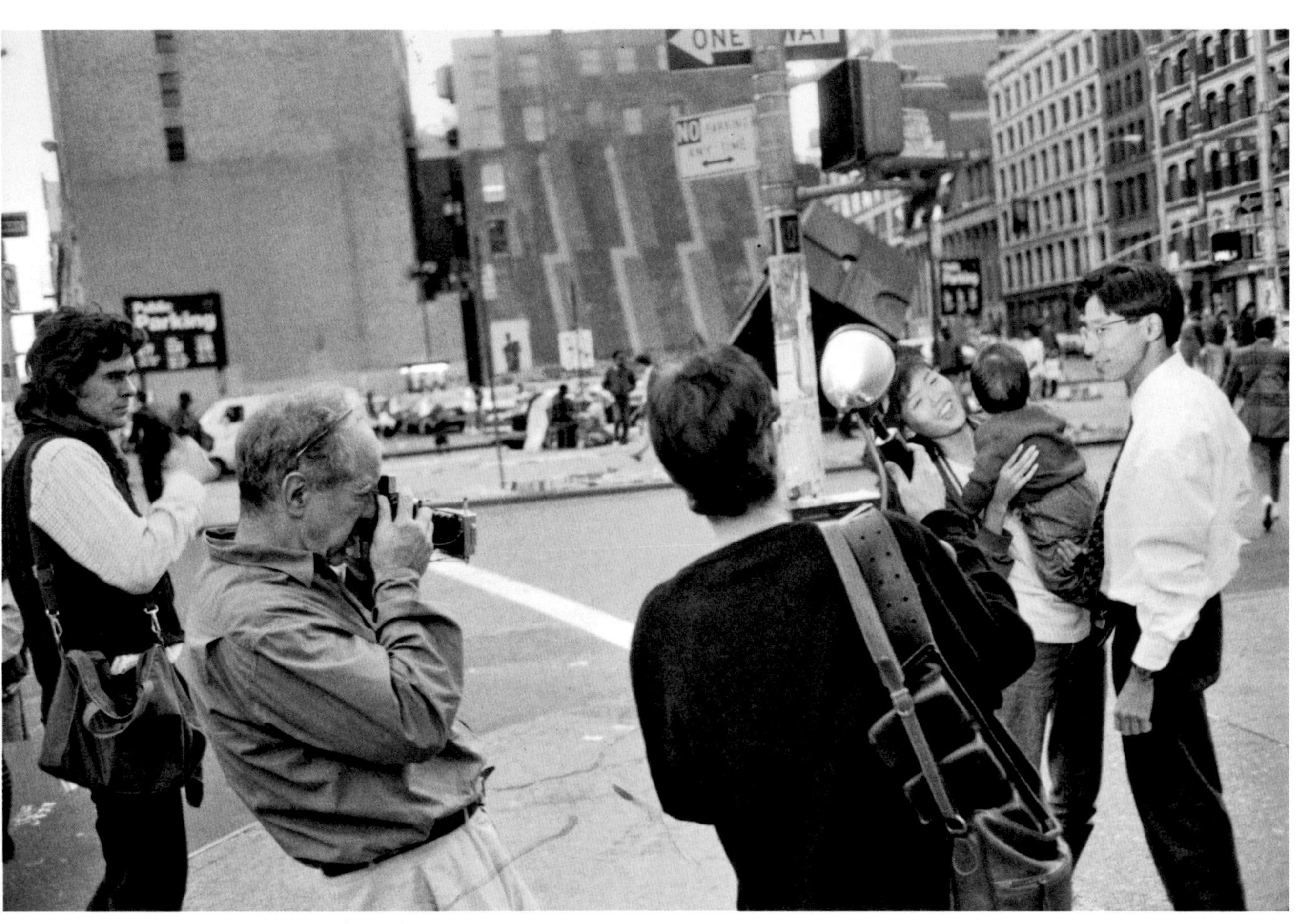

Robert returns to fashion to photograph an
Aspesi shirt collection, Astor Place, NYC, 1988

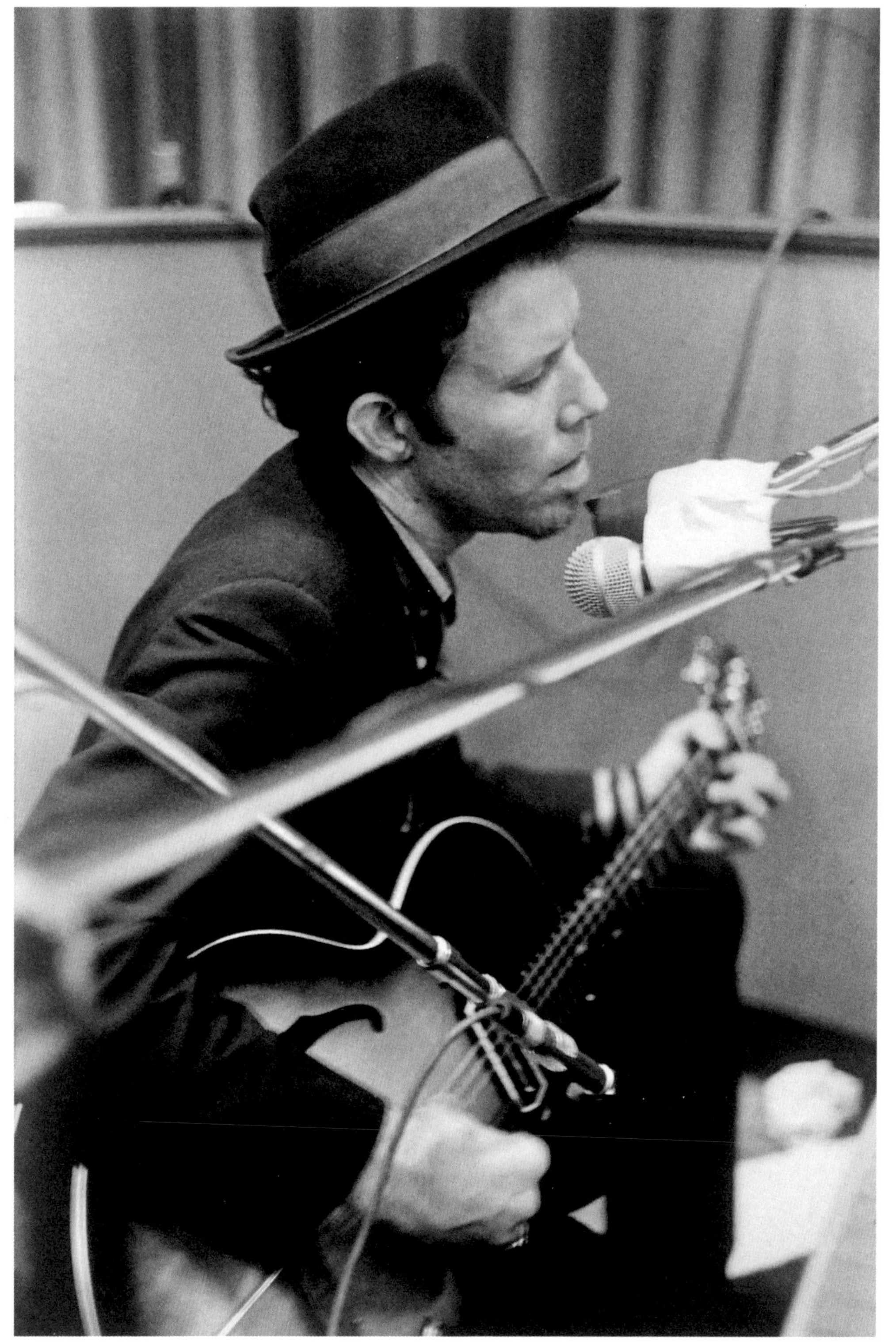

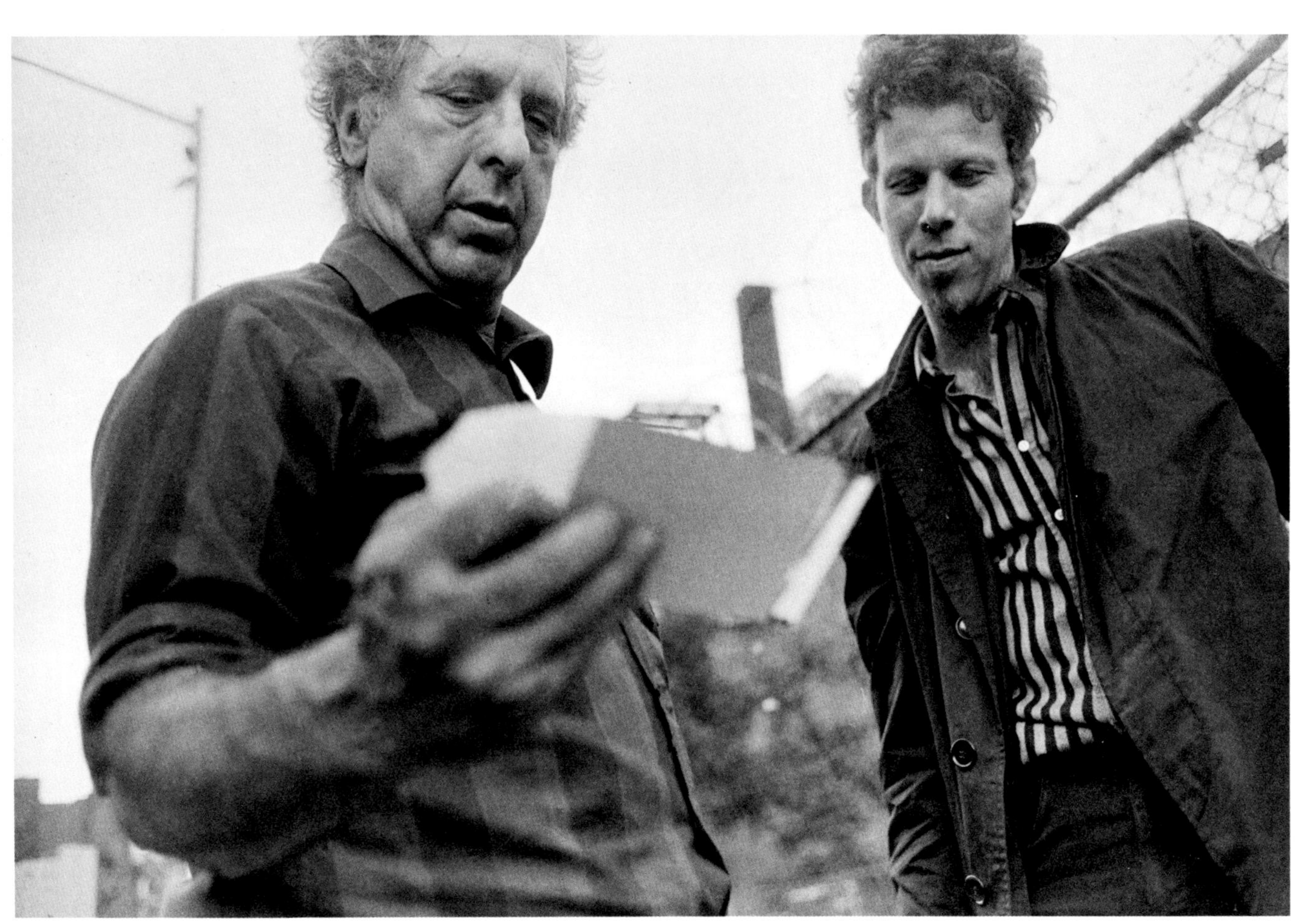

Visiting Tom Waits with Robert during
the recording of *Rain Dogs*, 1985

East 1ˢᵗ Street – Robert photographs Tom Waits
for the cover of *Rain Dogs*, 1985

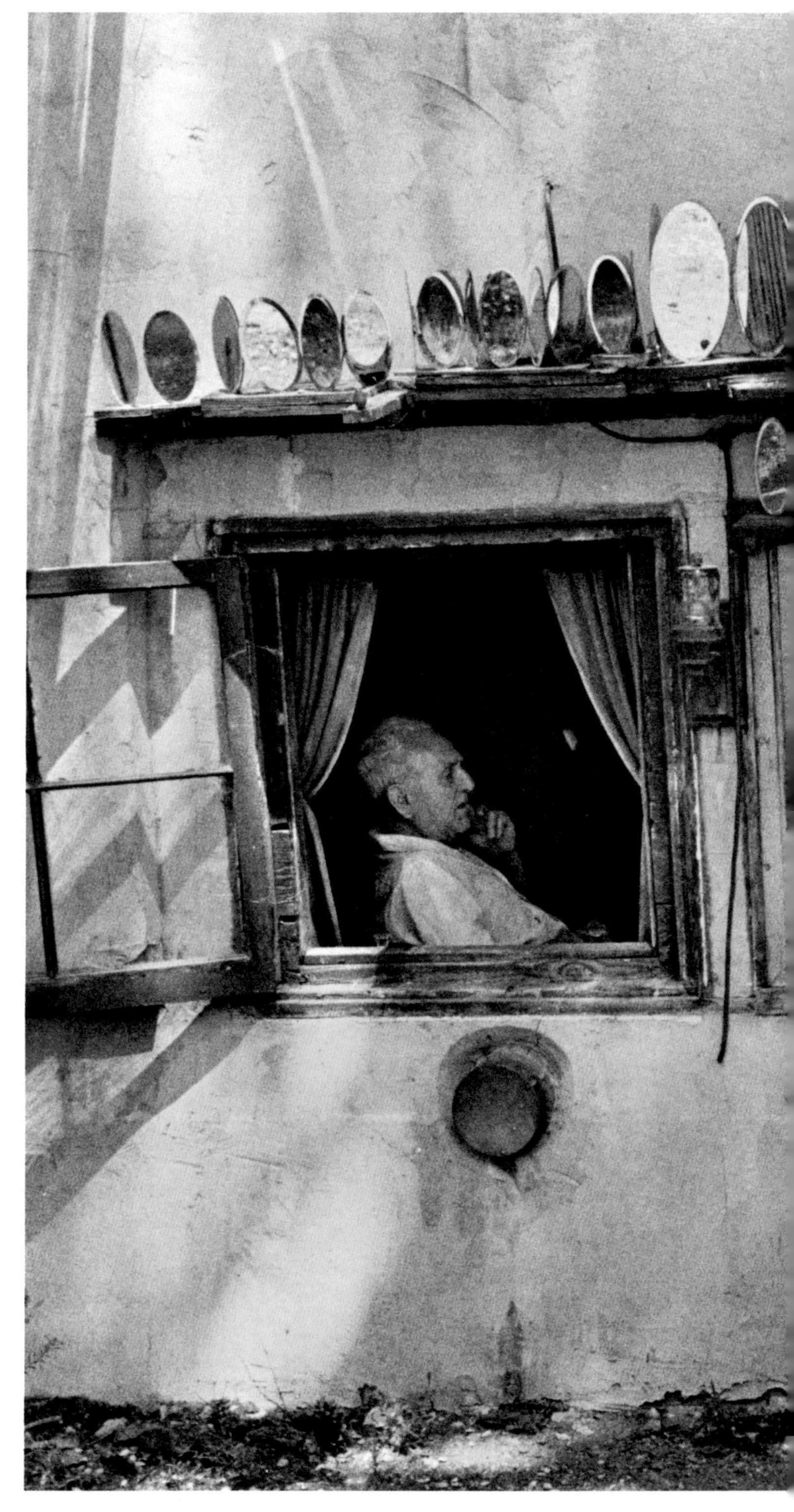

Raoul Hague's cabin,
Maverick Road, Woodstock, NY, 1988

Raoul was an abstract sculptor who was guru
and mentor to Robert, Lee Friedlander and
numerous other artists.

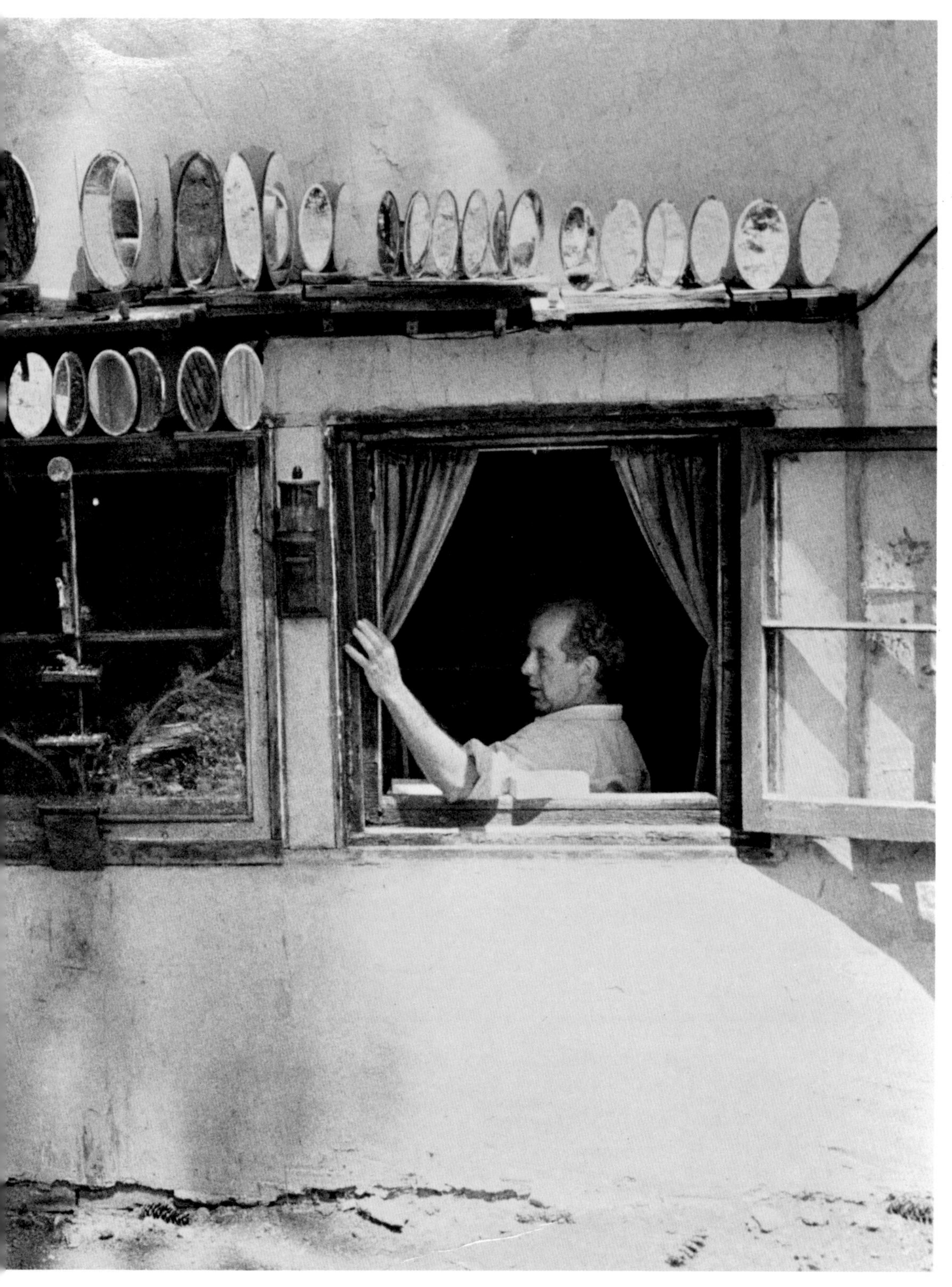

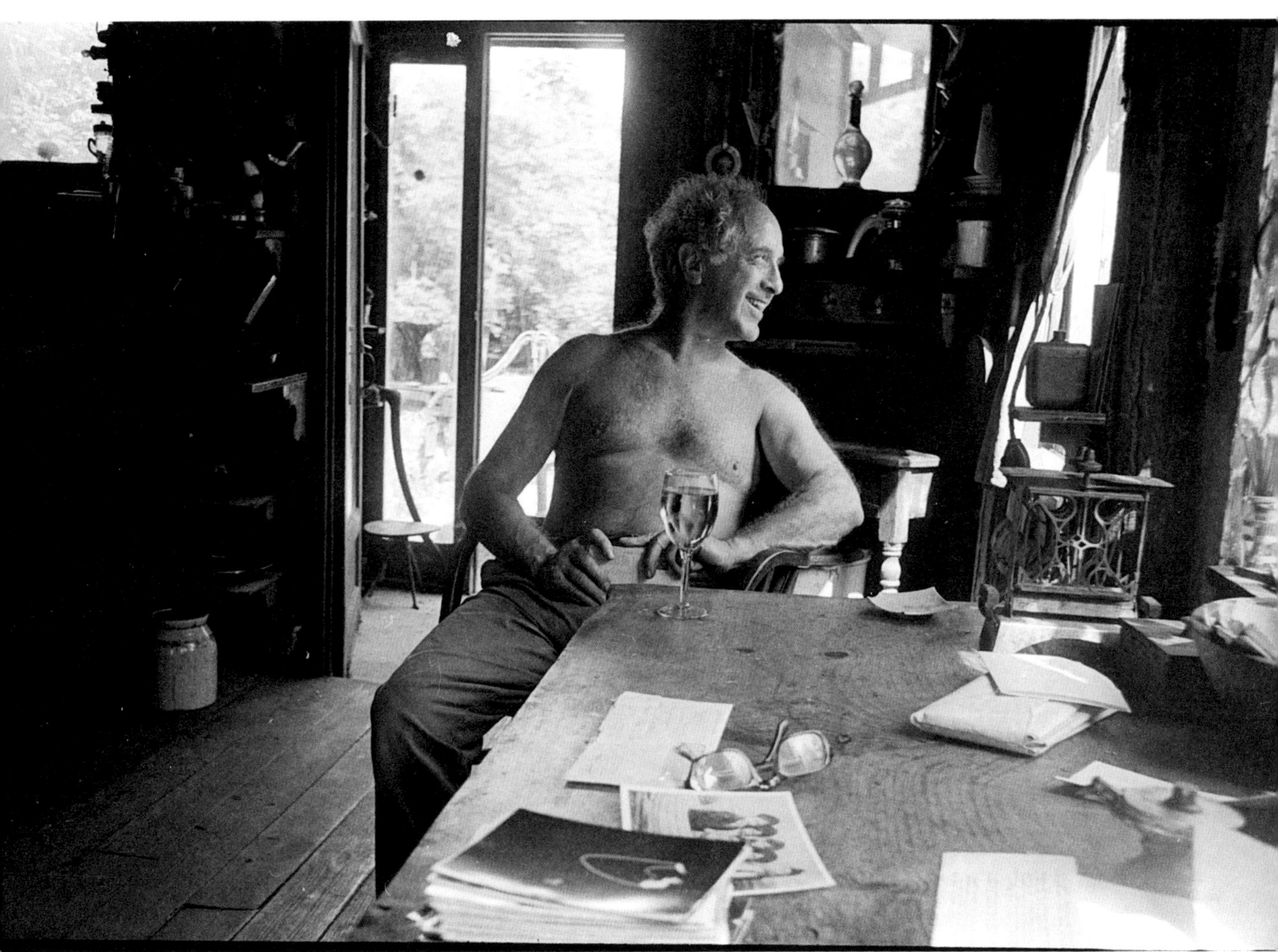

Robert at Raoul Hague's home, Maverick Road, Woodstock, NY, 1988

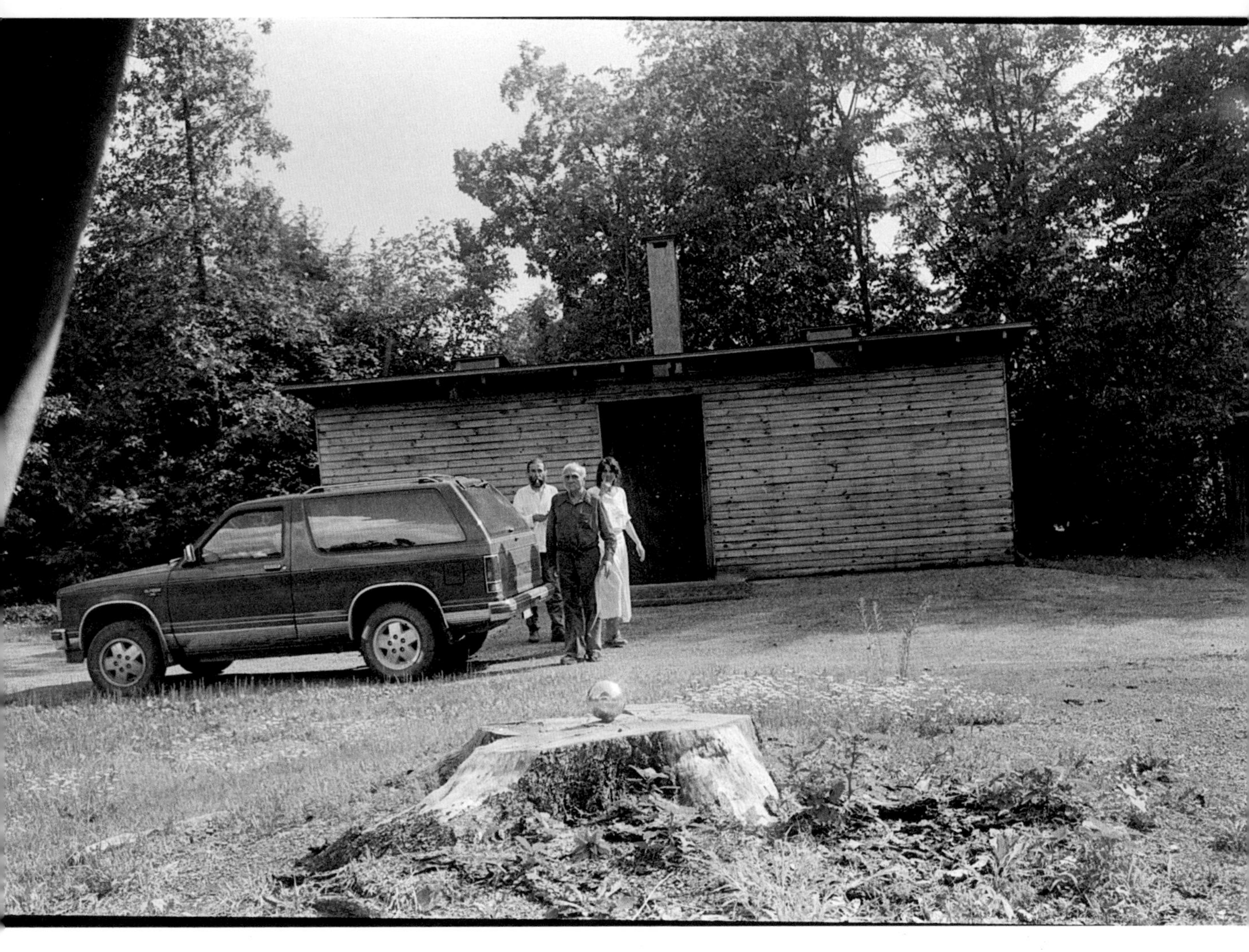

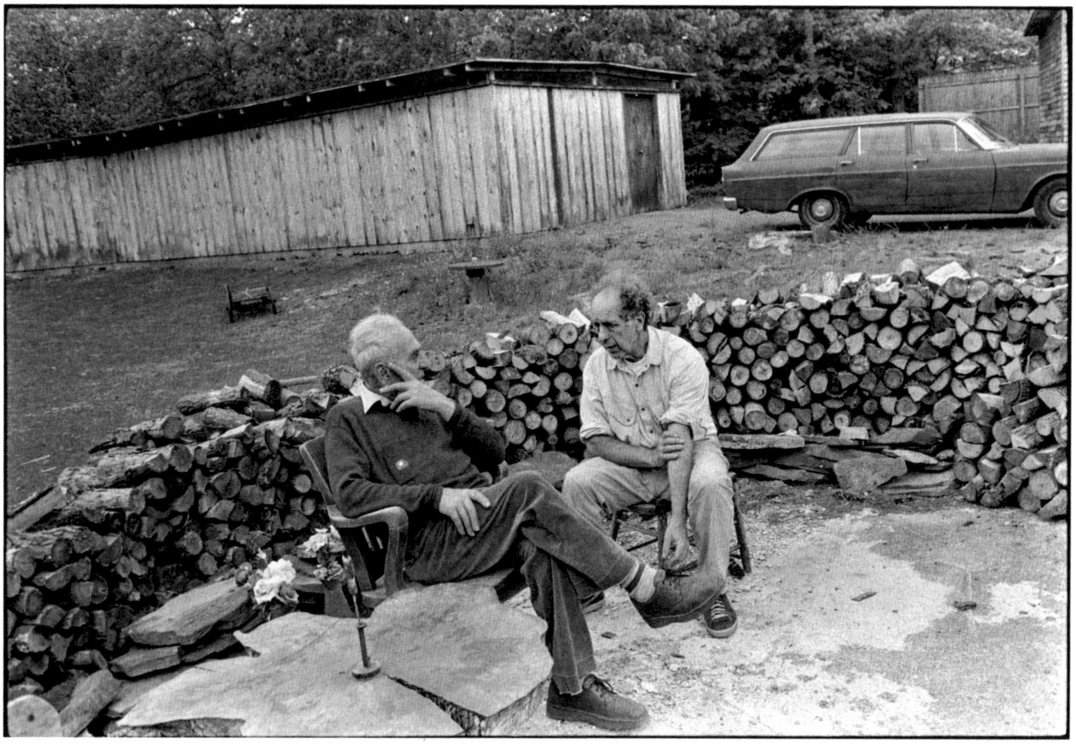

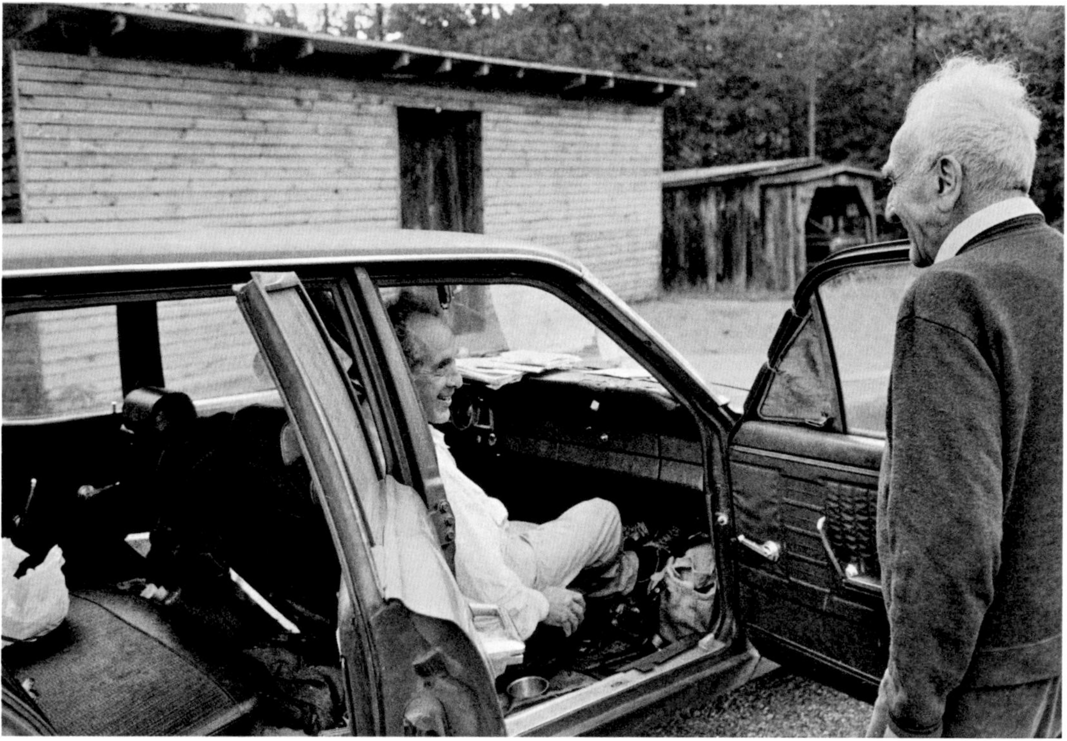

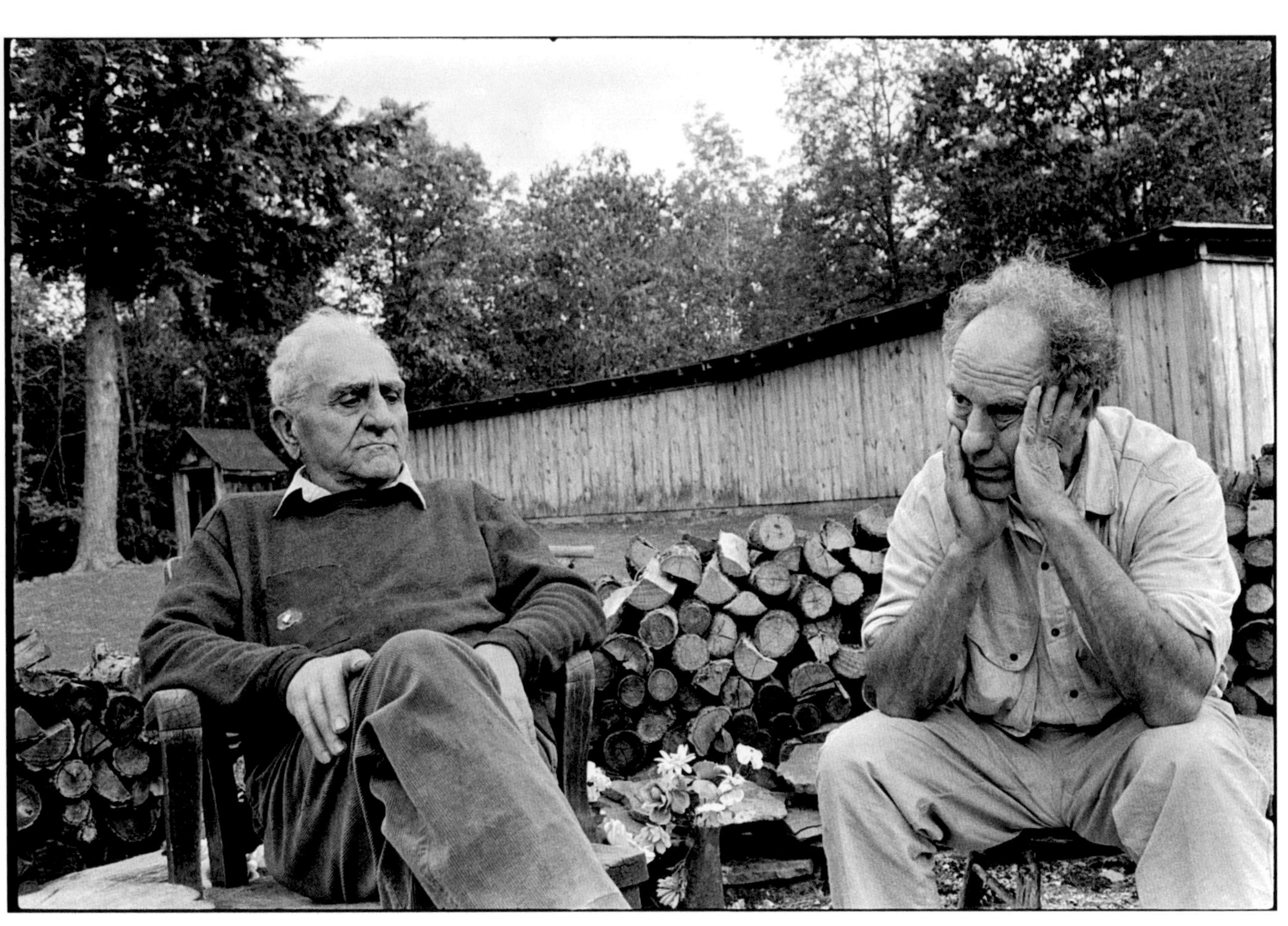

Hague and Robert, Maverick Road, Woodstock, NY, 1988

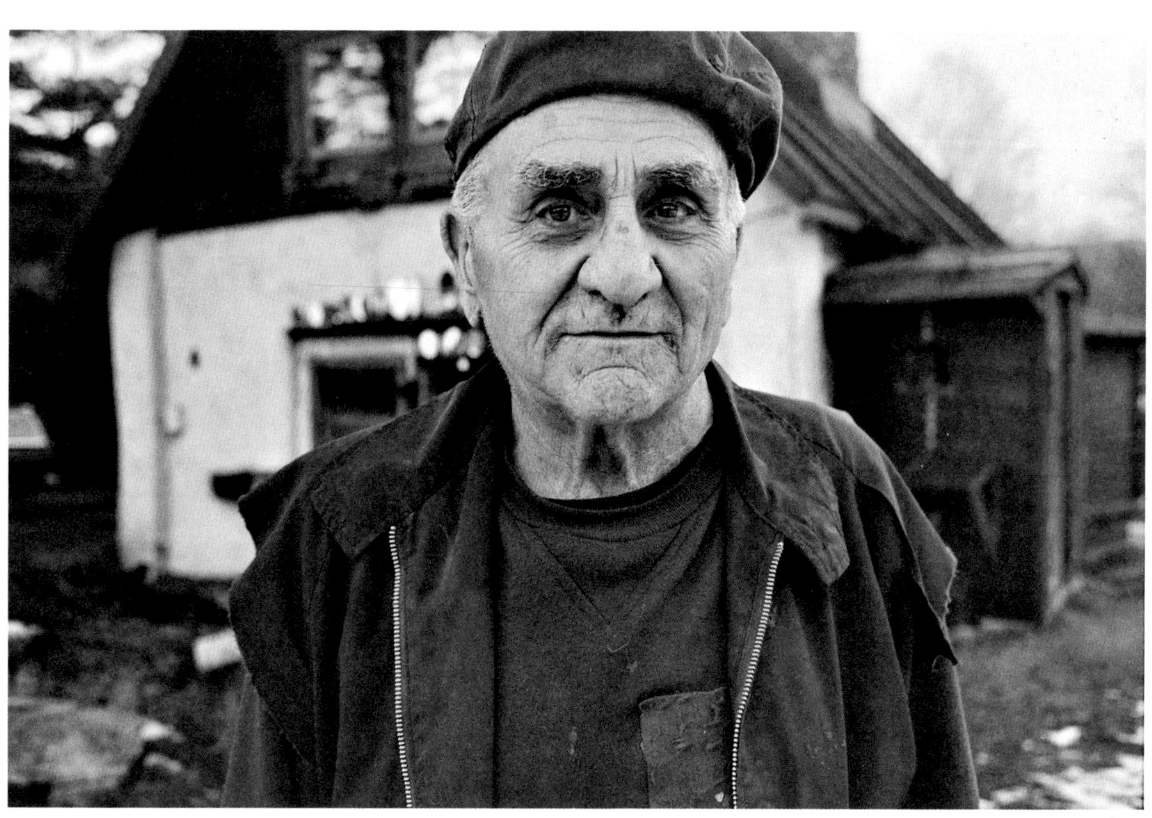

Raoul Hague, Woodstock, NY, 1988

SNOW GLOBE

Notebook, December 21ˢᵗ, 1987

On December nights like this one, cold and dark, on old Maverick Road, Woodstock, Hague would be out to libraries in New Paltz or Woodstock to read. He spoke a lot about how he would walk from Kingston (13 miles) to his cabin until he got his motorcycle and rode it all year long.

Raoul kept scrapbooks and enjoyed showing me pictures of snow storms taken around the time he returned home from his heart bypass surgery. The next day, I am back in New York and I imagine Hague forever in a snow globe. The previous night, Hague wondered if Sartre had ever read any of Jack London and said: "Tell Robert that."

Brian Graham

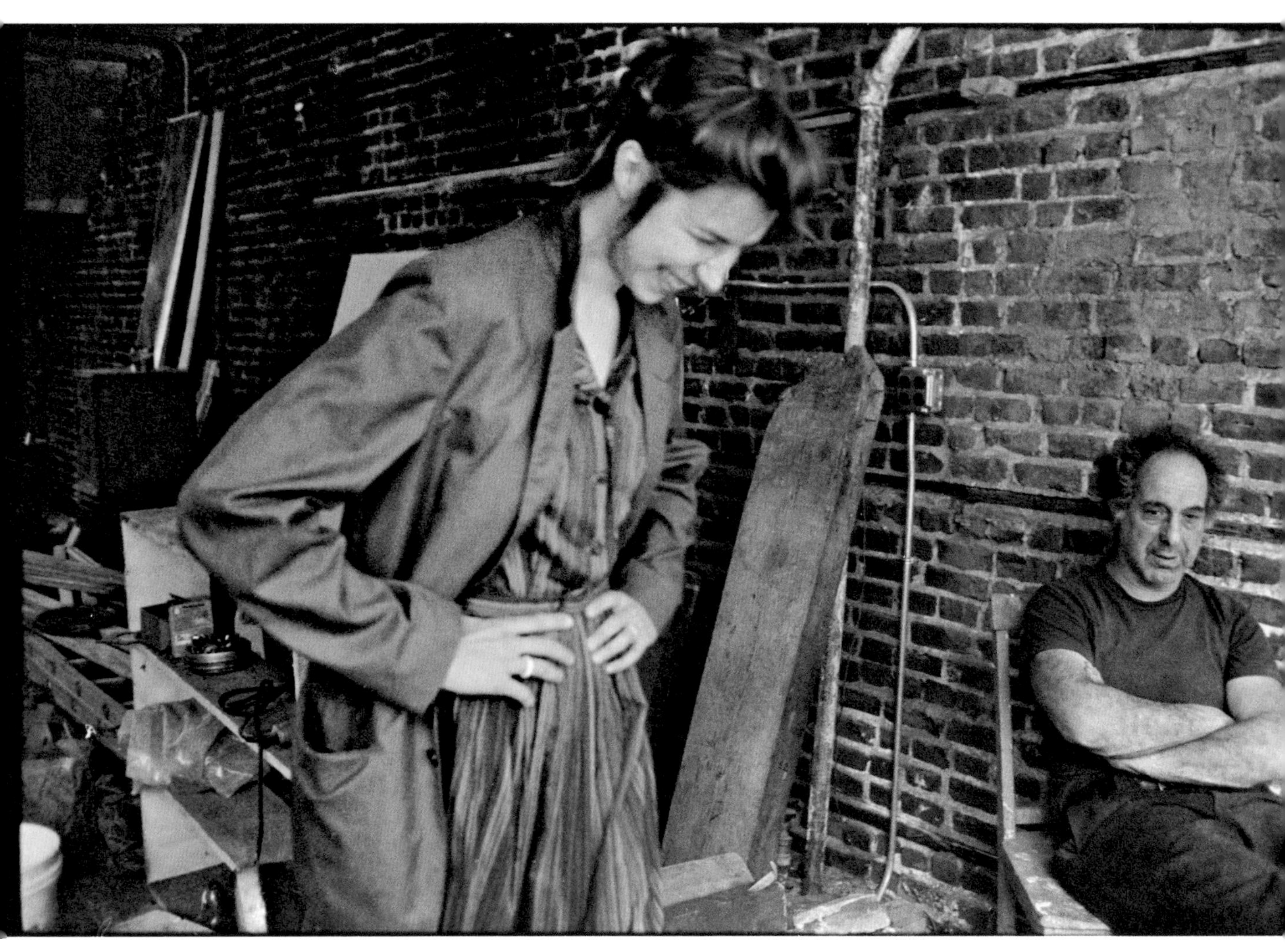

Sara Driver, Robert Frank, Jim Jarmusch and June Leaf at 7 Bleecker studio, 1983

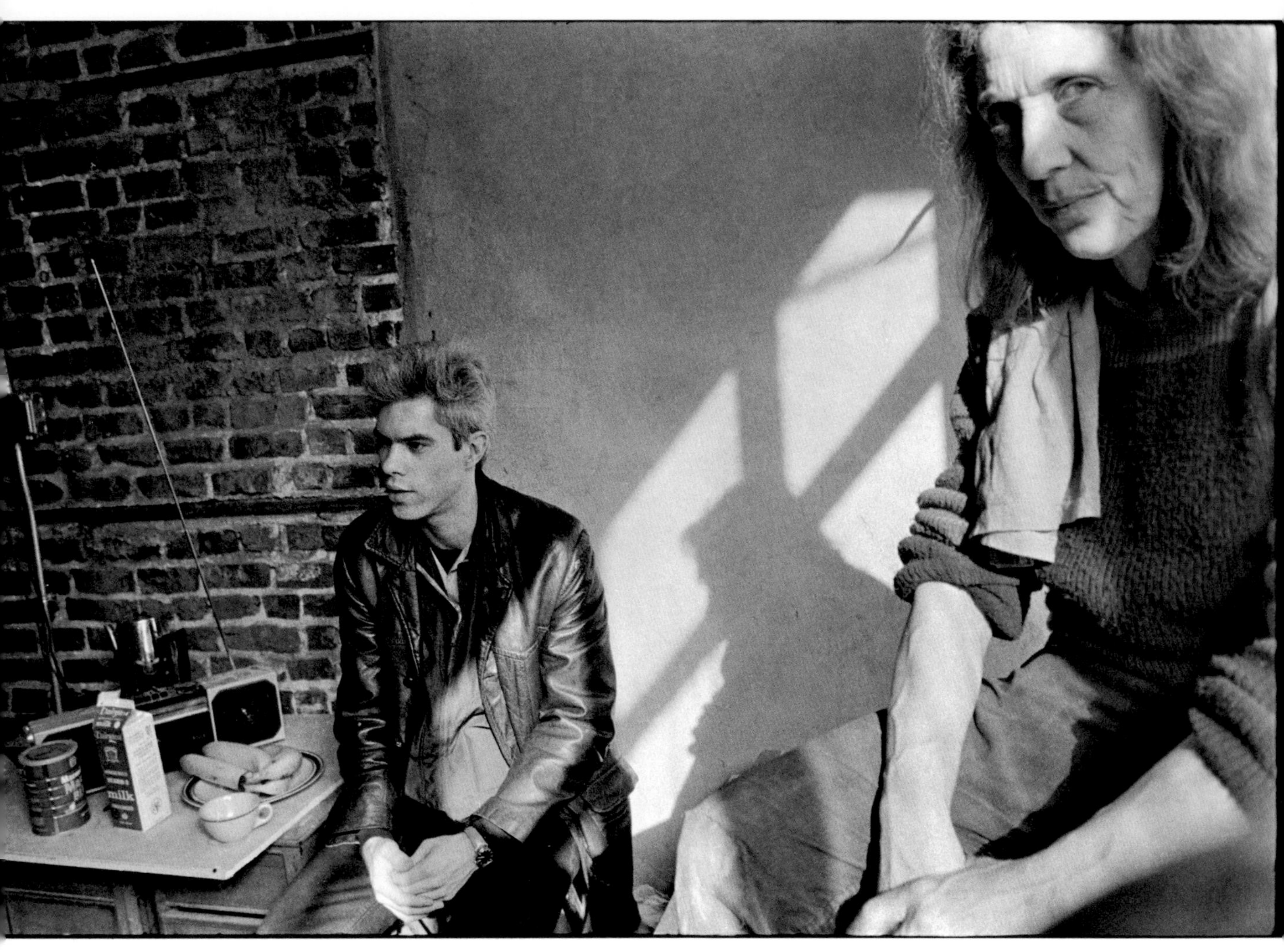

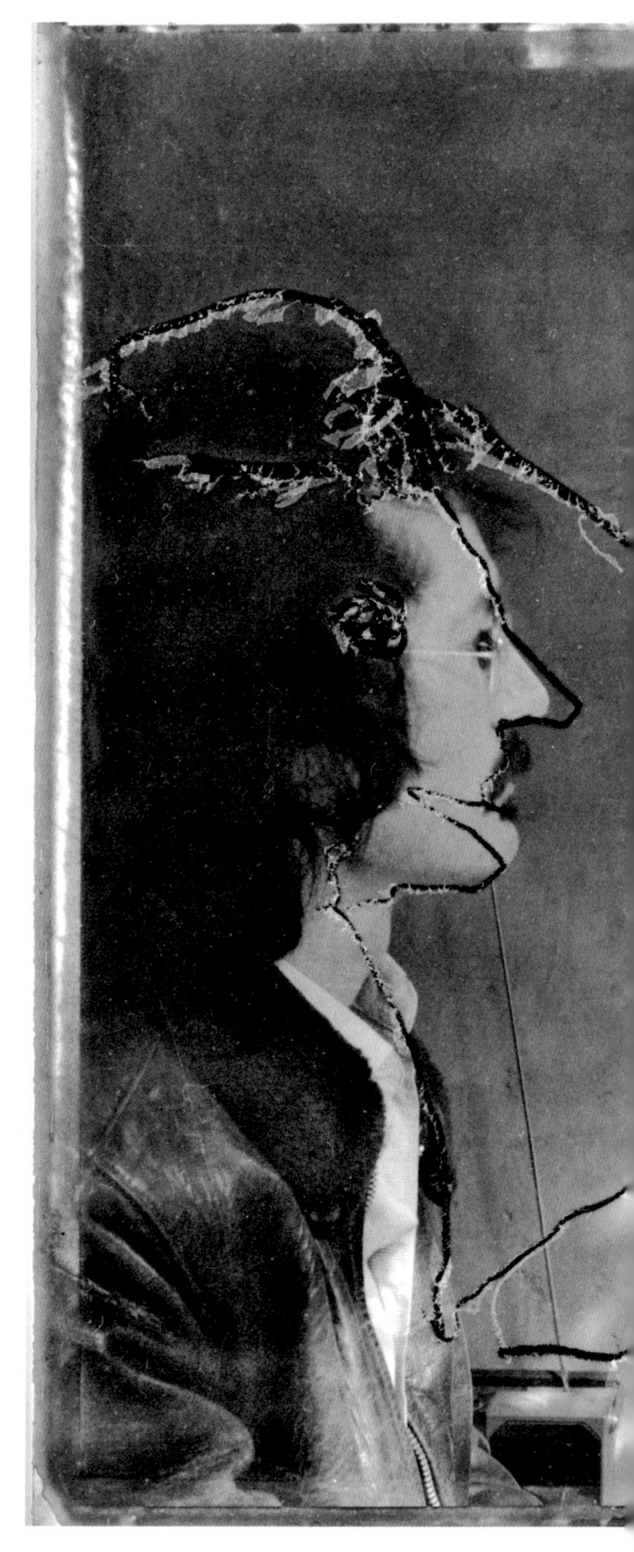

Self-portrait with Robert Frank,
(R.F. scratching on Polaroid negative), NYC, 1988

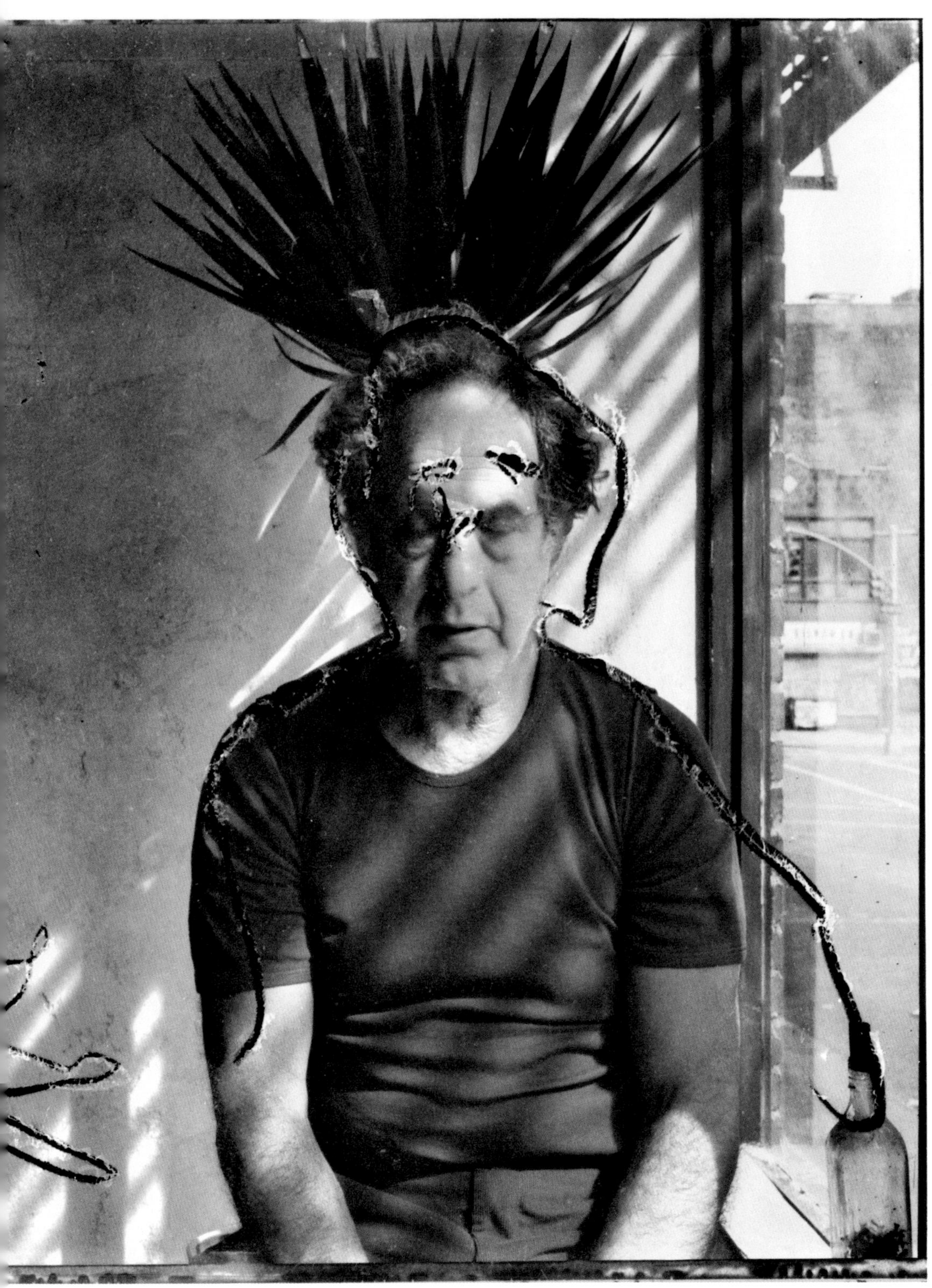

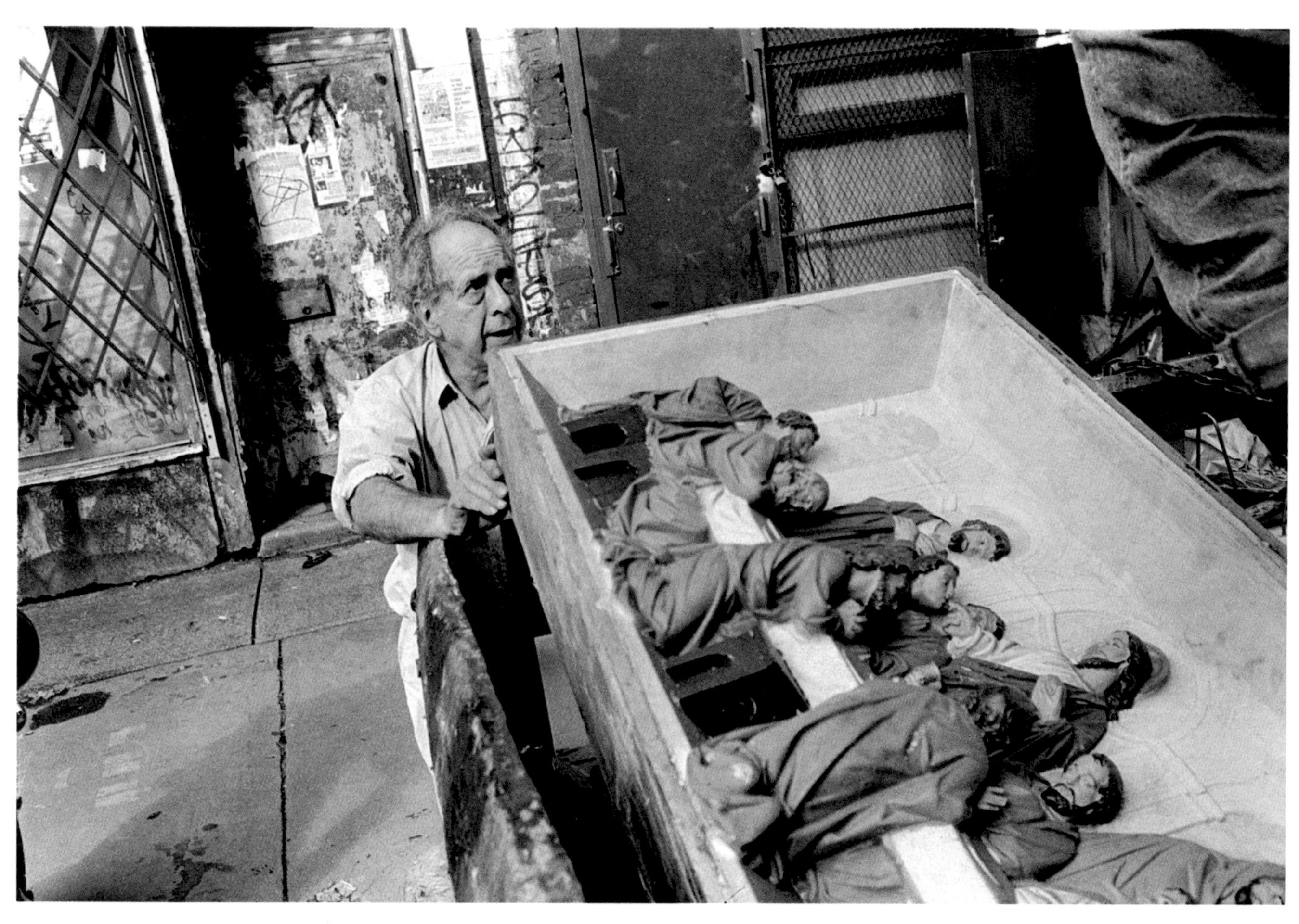

Robert with Harry Smith, 7 Bleecker Street, NYC, 1986

Harry was an ethnographic modernist who compiled and edited Smithsonian Folkways Recording's *Anthology of American Folk Music*.

Salvaged church relic, NYC, 1990

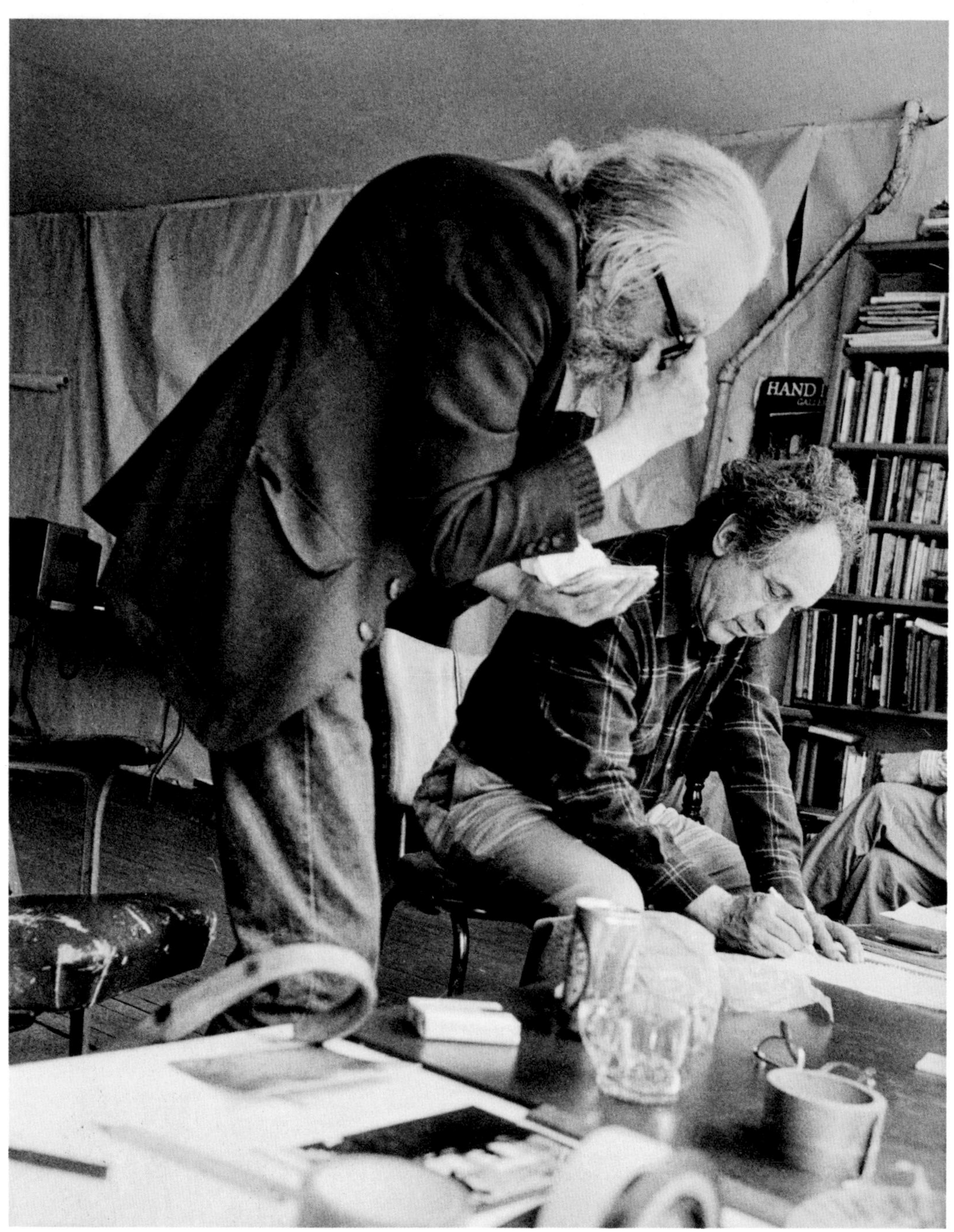

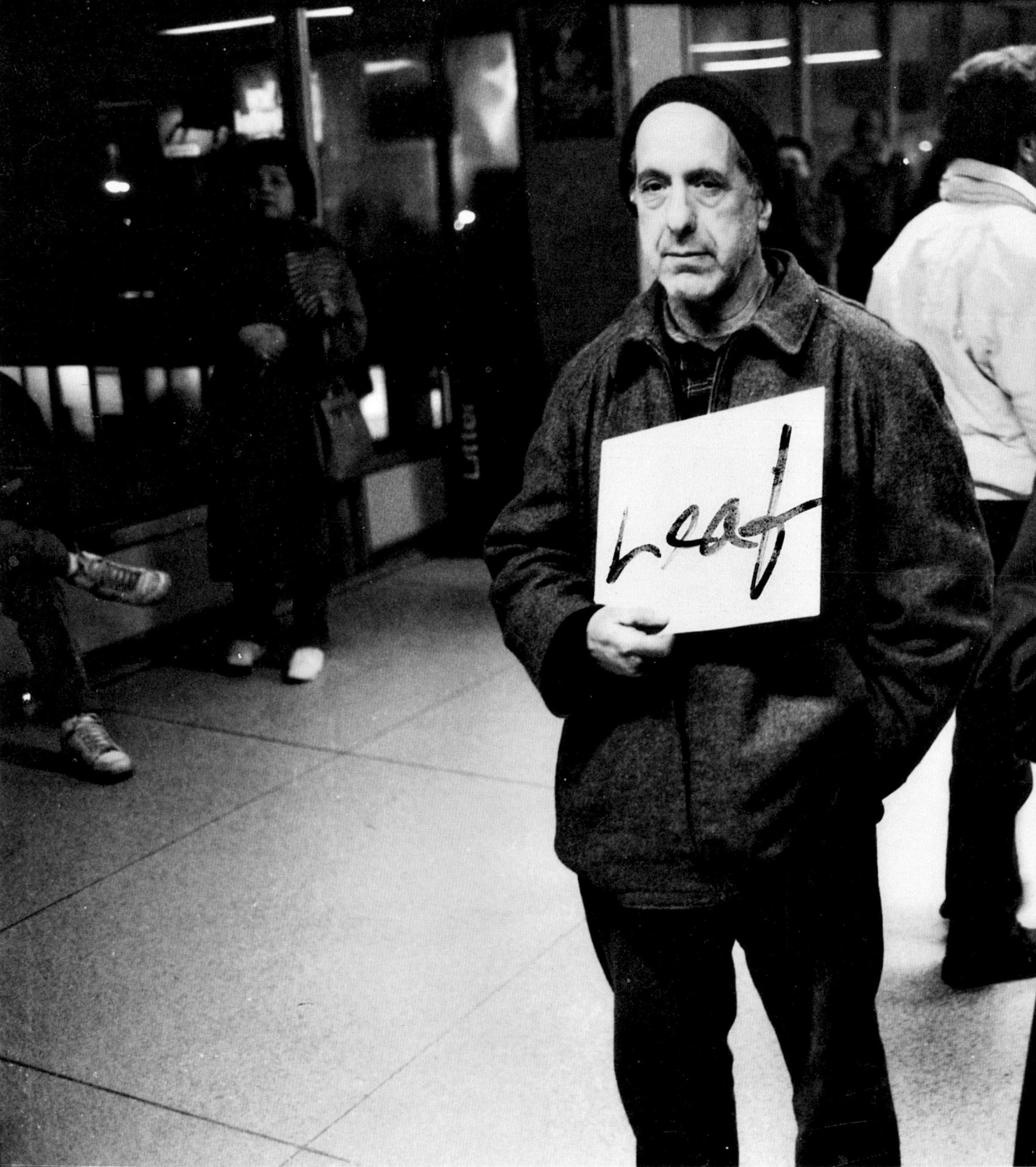
Leaf

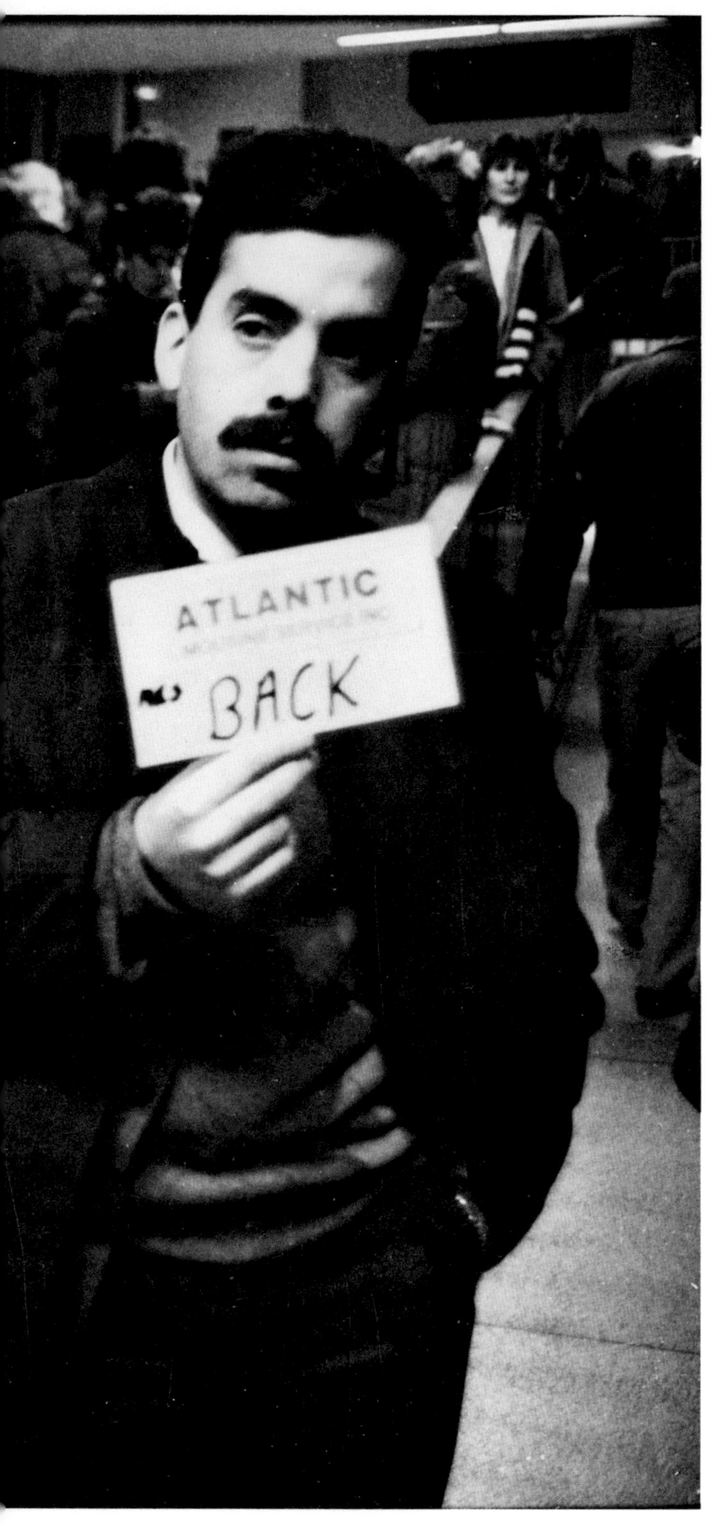

Newark Airport arrivals, 1984

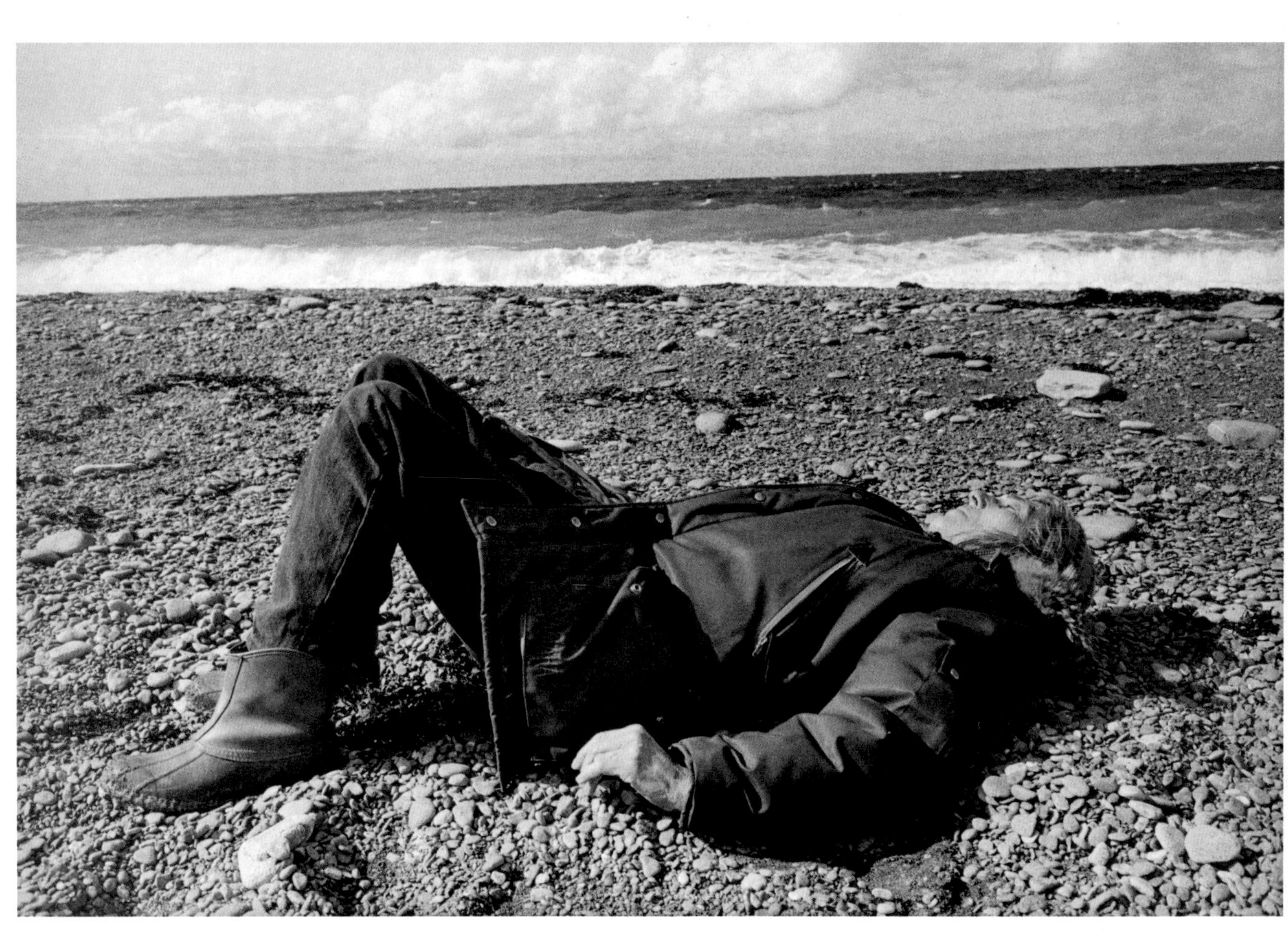

June Leaf, Mabou Mines, 1992

7 Bleecker Street, 2002

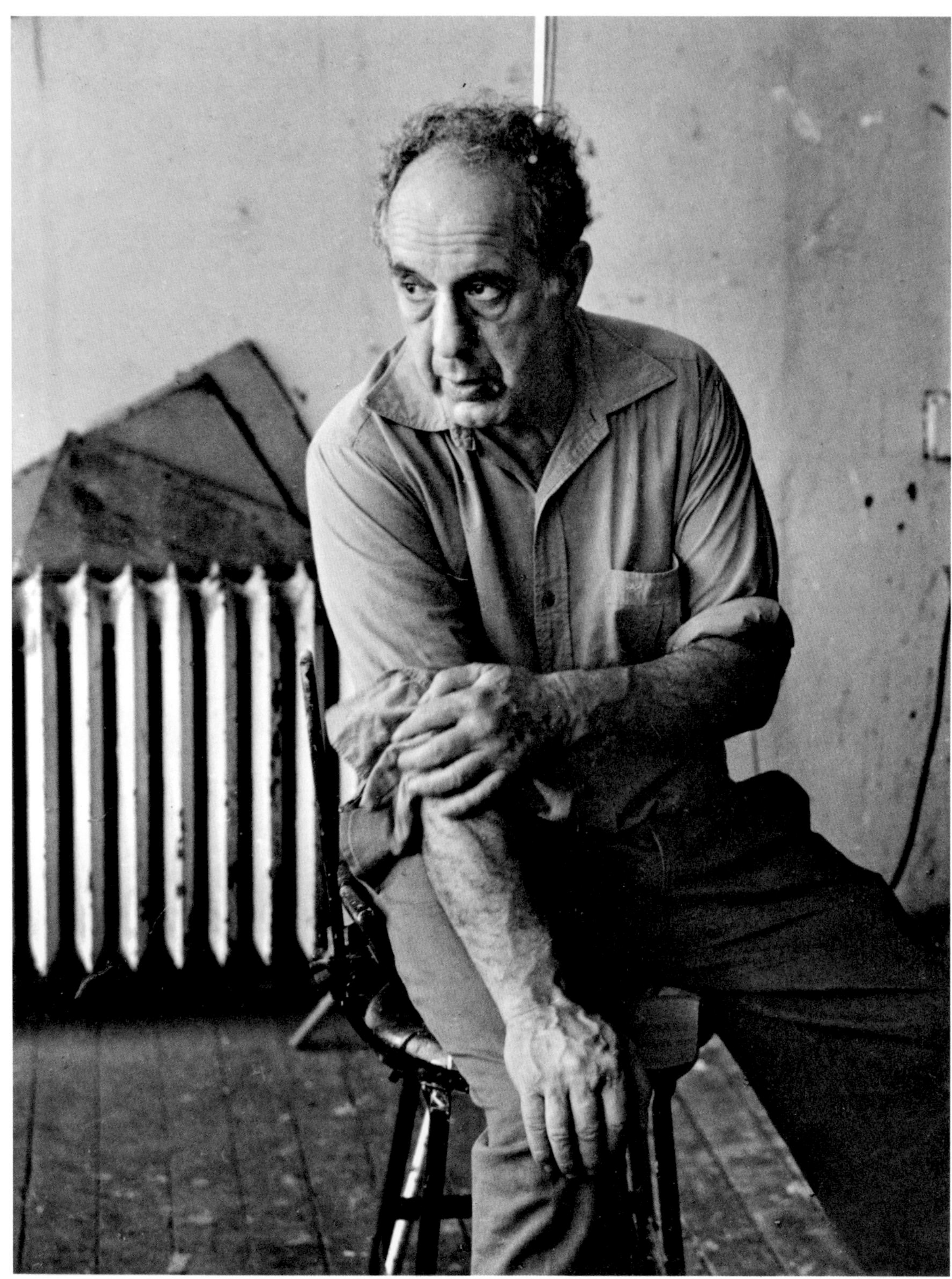

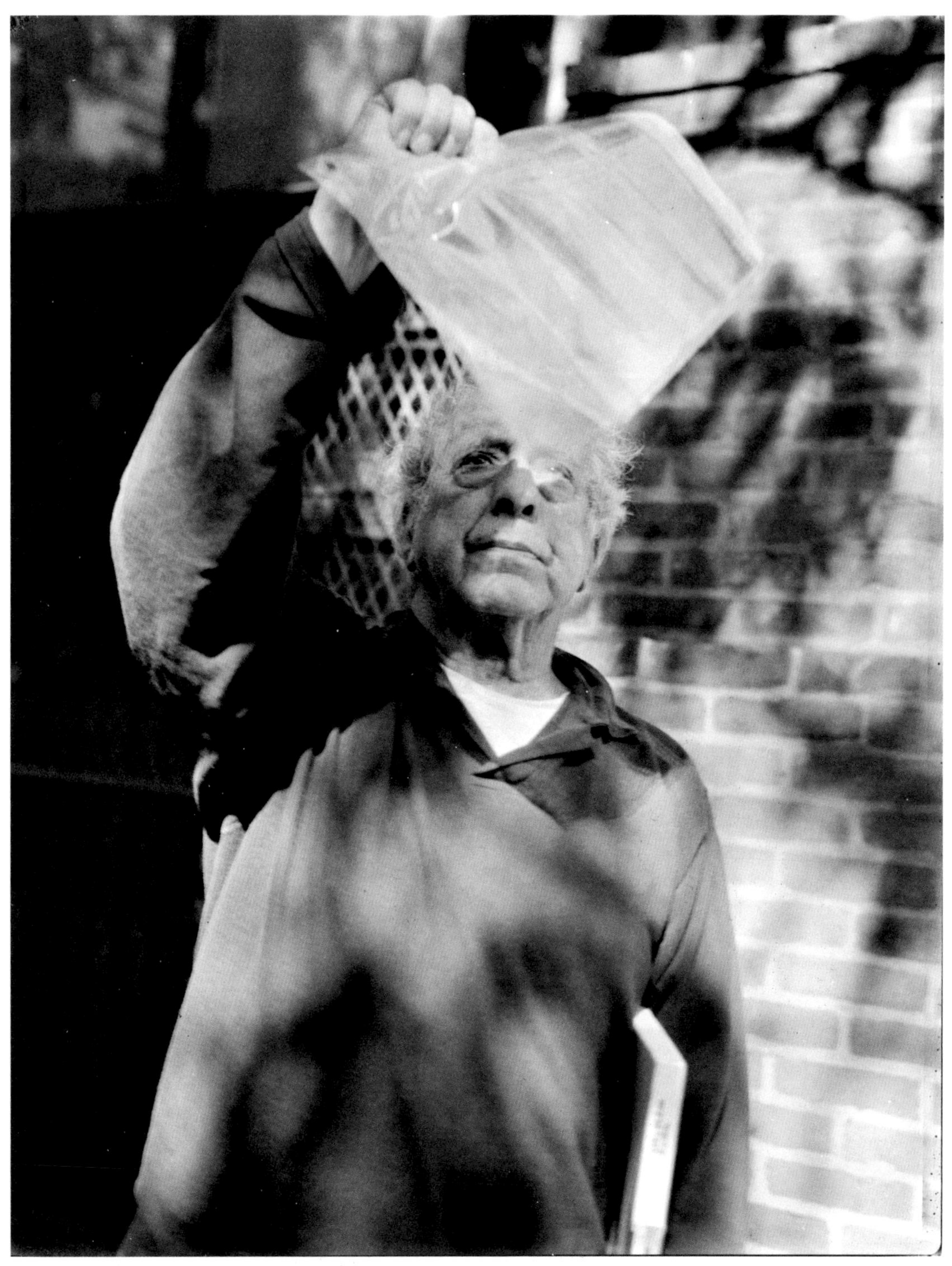

Sheet of negatives, 7 Bleecker Street, 2007

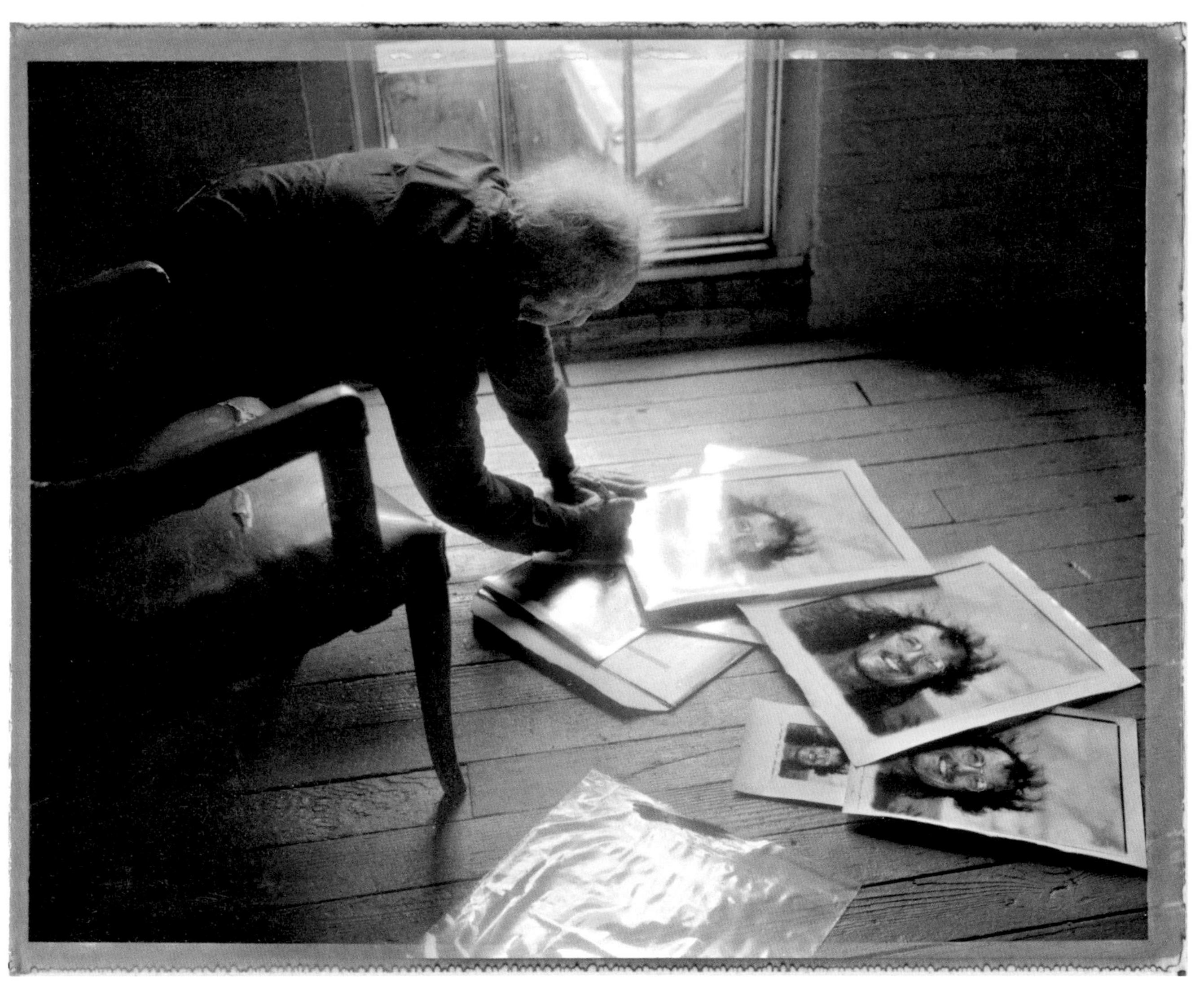

Signing prints, Newark, NJ, 2002

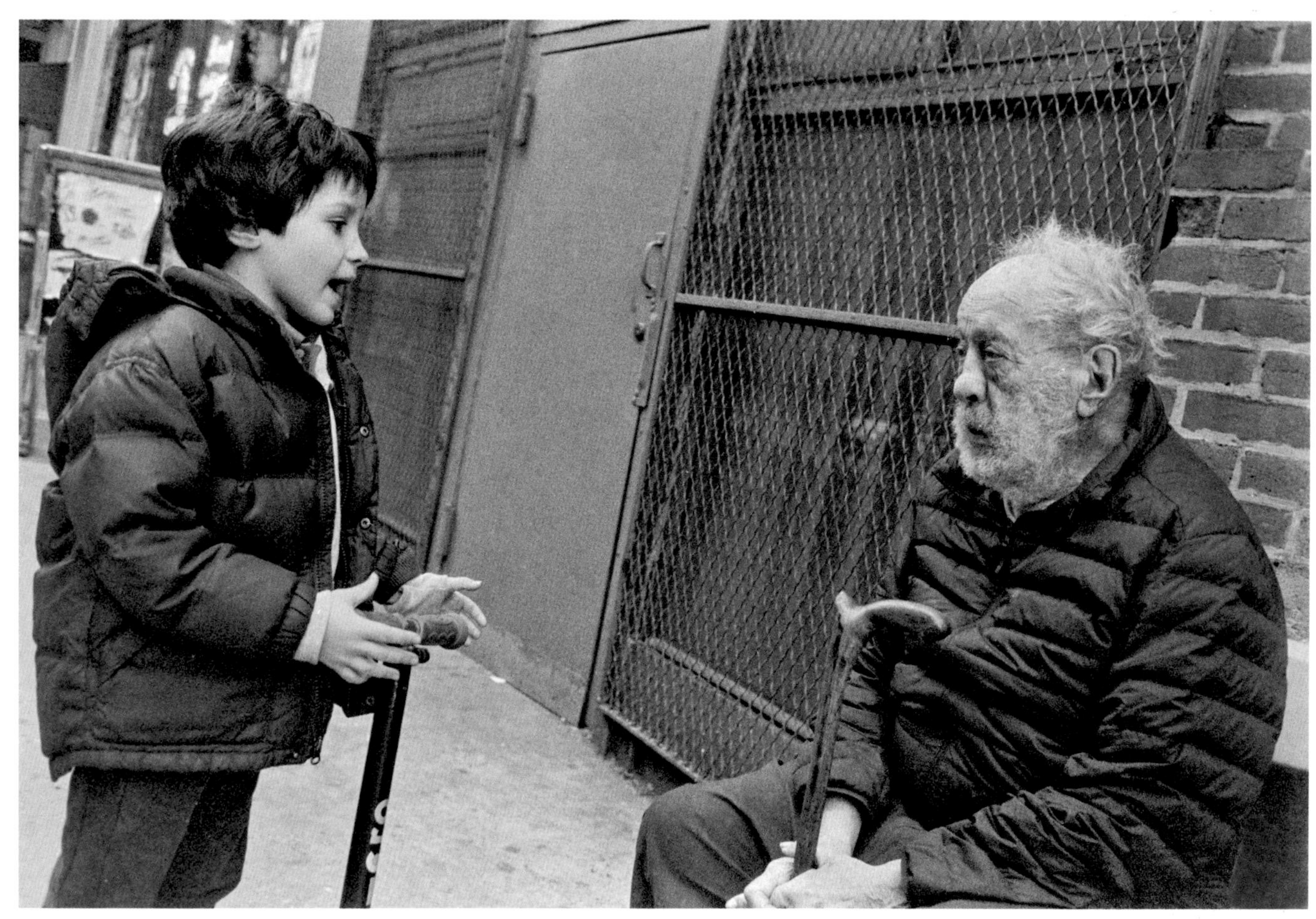

Adrien Graham and Robert outside 7 Bleecker Street, 2019

June Leaf, Adrien Graham and Robert
outside 7 Bleecker Street, 2018

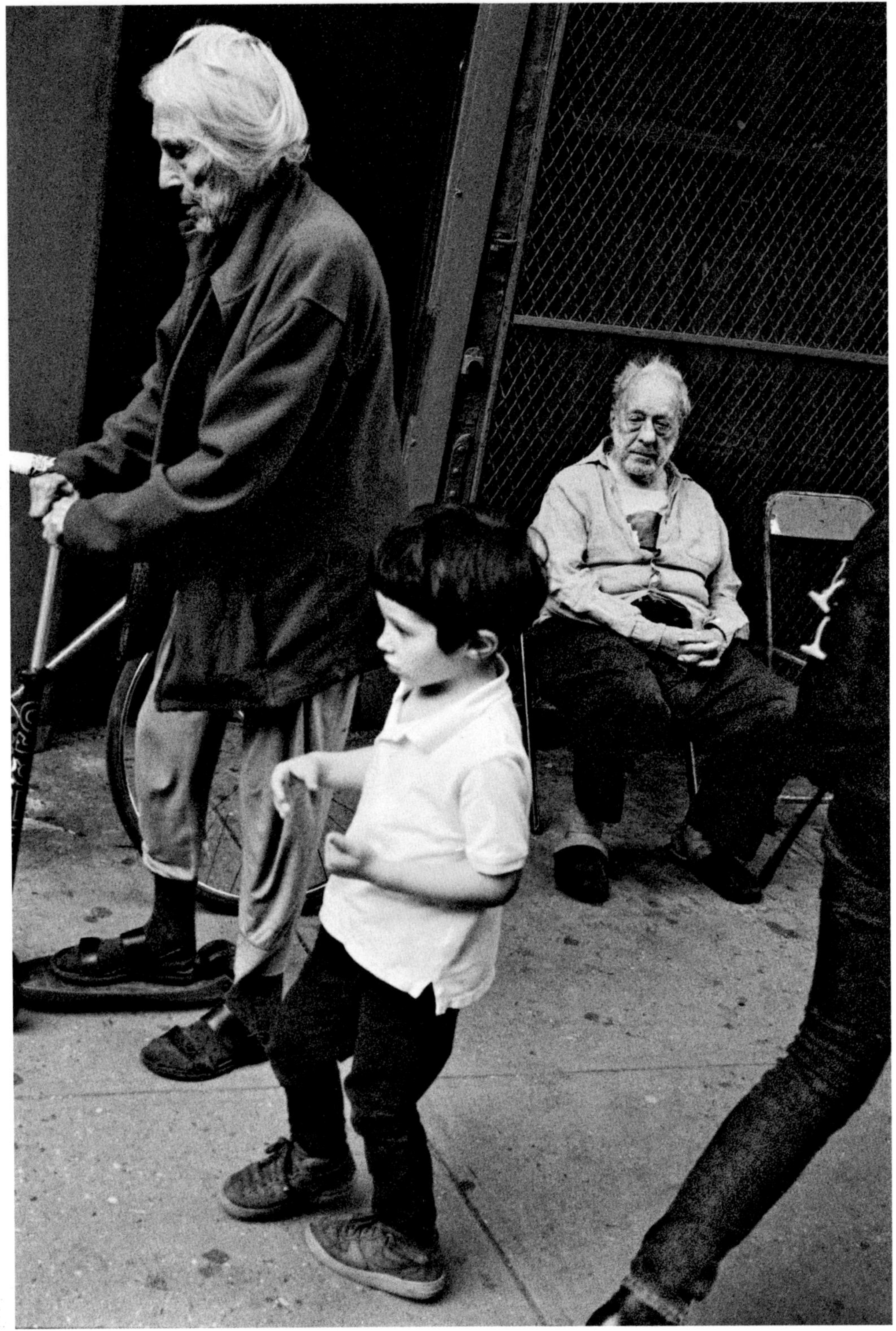

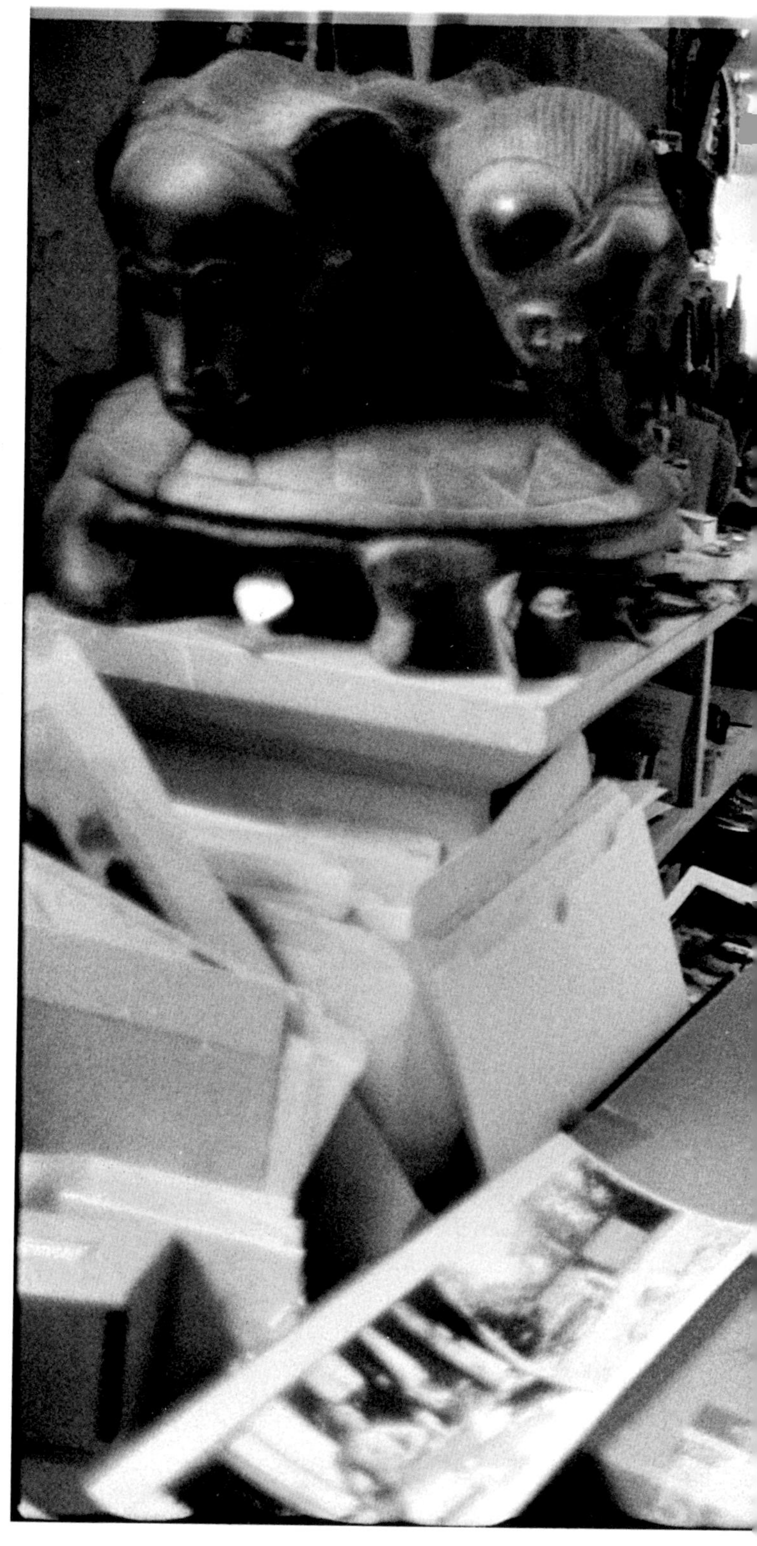

Robert and his assistant Ayumi Furuta,
7 Bleecker Street, 2017

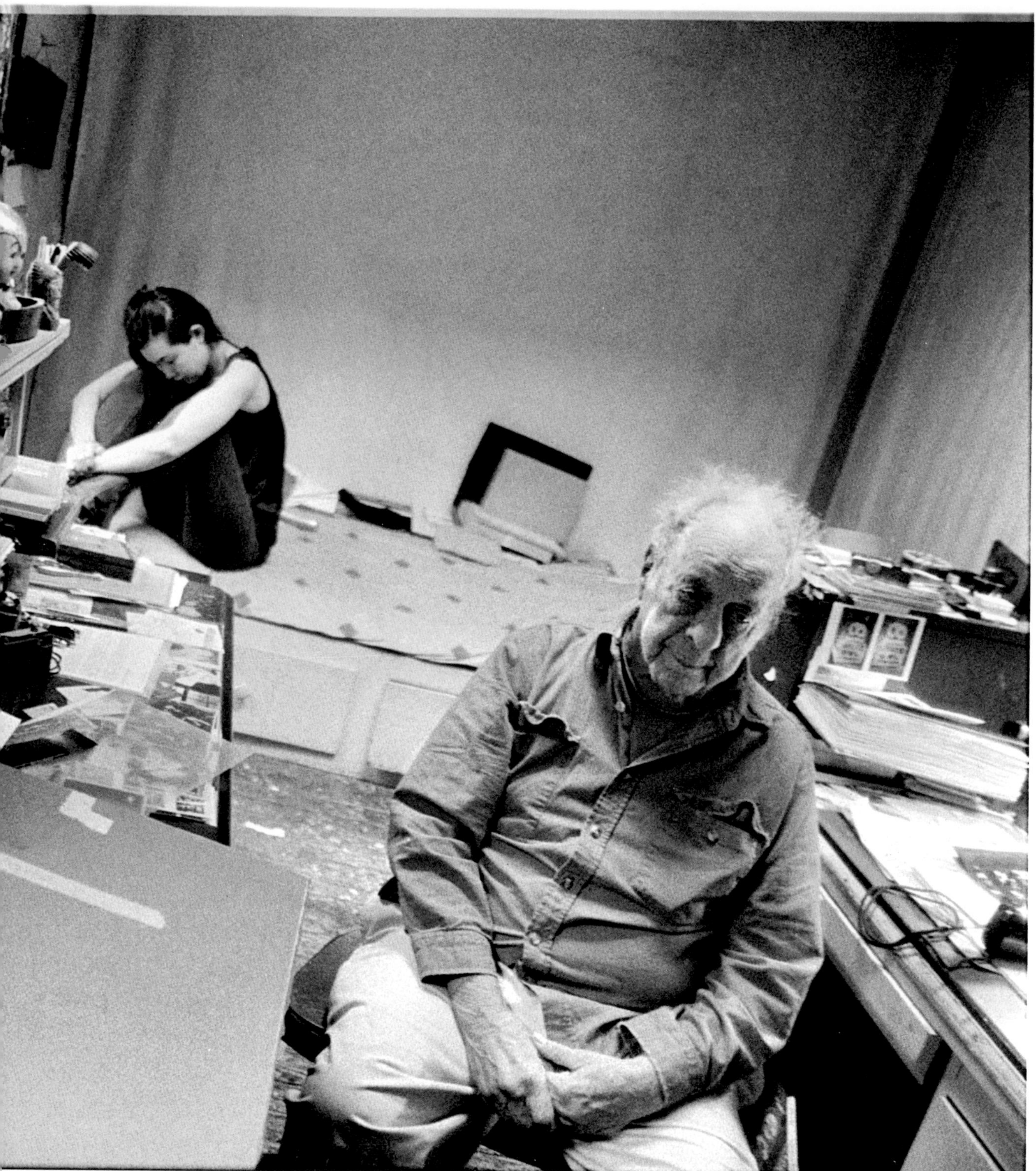

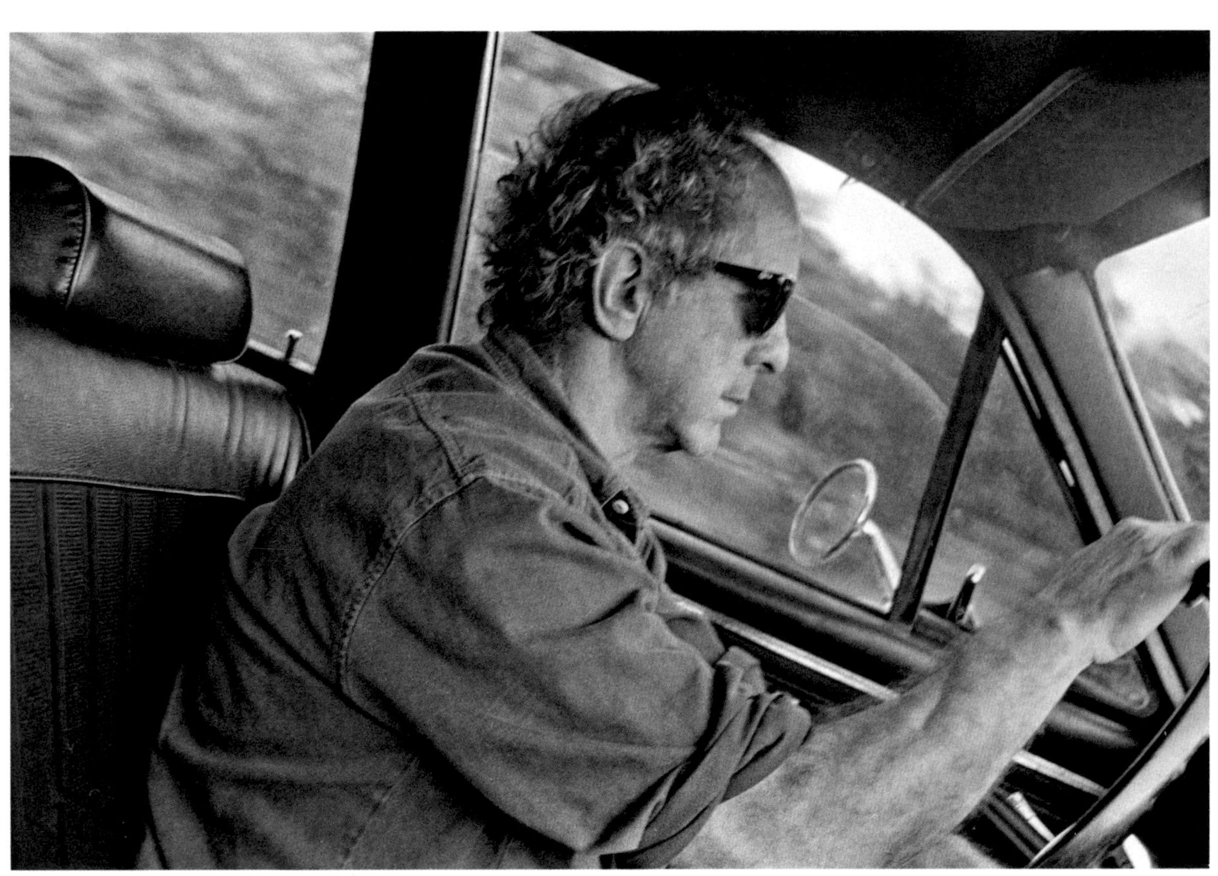

Ford Falcon, Route 207, New York State, 1992

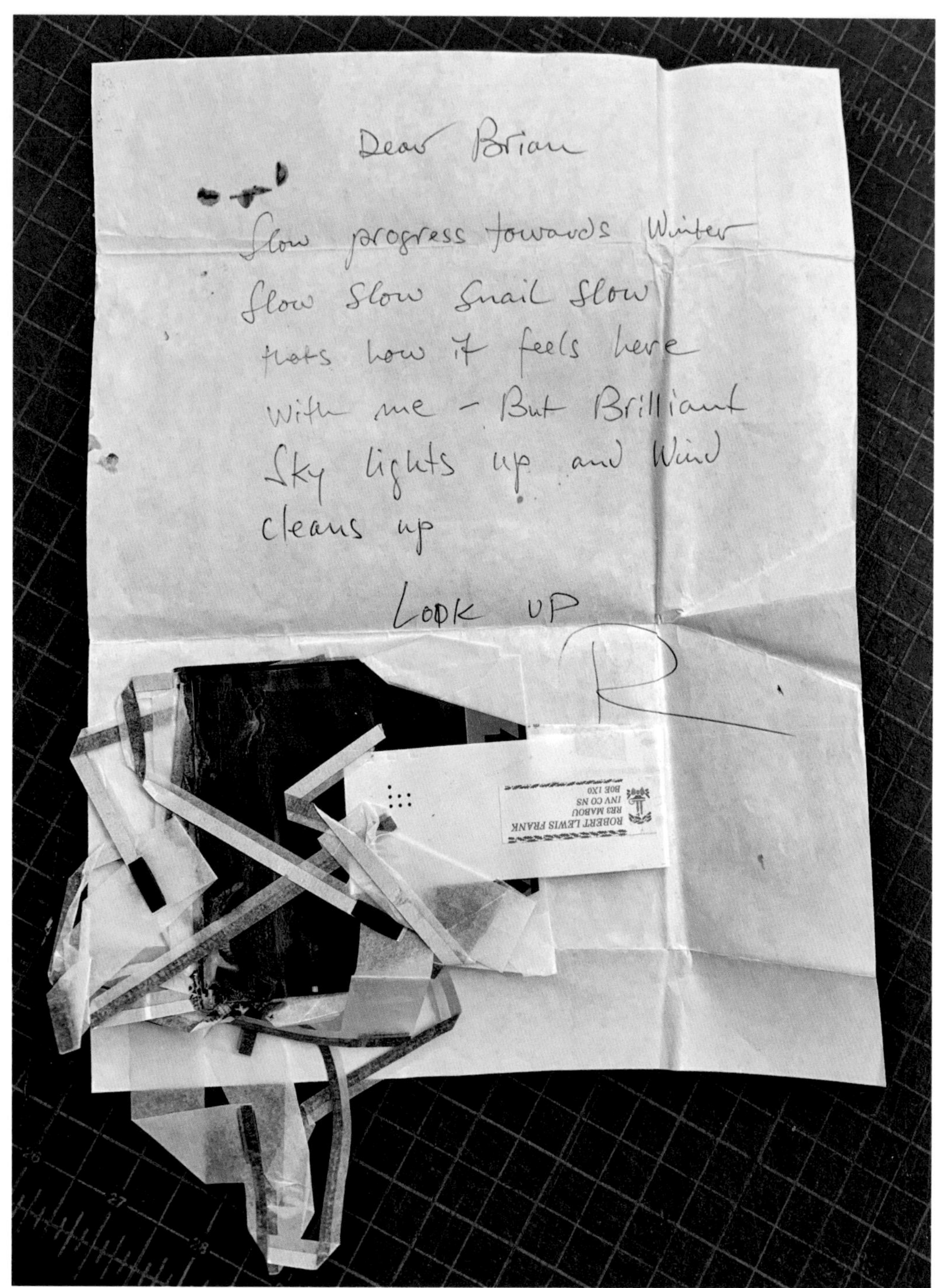

Note from Robert, 1985

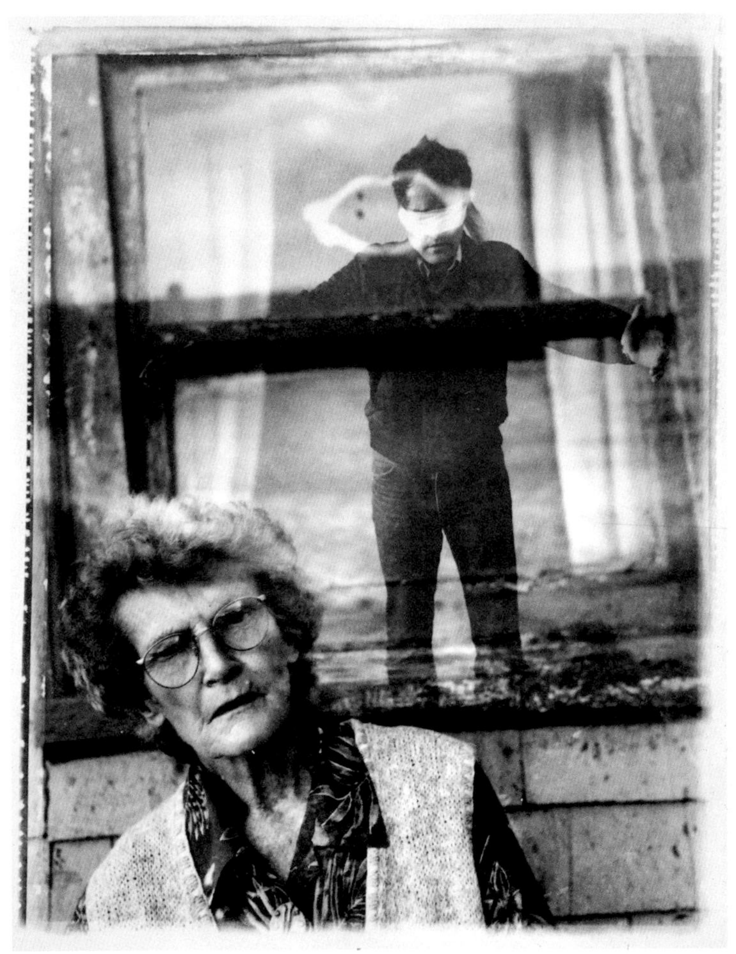

"Good morning heartache
Here we go again
Might as well get used to you hanging around
Good morning heartache
Sit down"

Billie Holiday

For my mother Colleen

Acknowledgments

Thanks to June Leaf for caring from the beginning. To my wife Emilie for starting this book with me, collecting images and editing them over the years. John T. Hill, photographer, editor and teacher, who co-designed the book with me and did the majority of the scanning work. Thanks to friends. John Parlante and Geoff Lawrence who have helped in editing the words and pictures in this book. Ed Grazda, photography's ambassador to the world. Gary Leon Hill, a master observer and recorder of spoken word, for nights of Johnny Cash while rifling through those photographs from Lincoln, Nebraska, and Paco Grande, our appointed Minister of Leisure by Robert. Thanks to Rudy Wurlitzer who set a new stretch of blacktop for this book to gain traction. I want to praise Ai Weiwei for stepping up as a friend and colleague thirty years after our last contact. Final thanks to Pauline Ahlstrom for her suggestions on finishing touches.

Born in Glace Bay, Canada, in 1951, Brian Graham earned his Bachelor of Arts from St. Francis Xavier University, Nova Scotia, in 1973. He moved to New York in 1981 to pursue photography and there assisted and printed for Robert Frank for more than a decade. He also printed the archives of Allen Ginsberg (chronicling the Beat years), the Walker Evans Estate and Rosalind Fox Solomon. Graham has photographed throughout Africa, Europe and the Americas, and exhibited in New York, Berlin and Lisbon.

First edition published in 2023

© 2023 Brian Graham for his photographs
© 2023 the authors for their texts
© 2023 Steidl Publishers for this edition

All rights reserved. No part of this publication may
be reproduced or transmitted in any form or by any
means, electronic or mechanical, including photocopy,
recording or any other storage and retrieval system,
without prior permission in writing from the publisher.

Book design: John T. Hill and Brian Graham
Scans and separations by Steidl image department

Production and printing: Steidl, Göttingen

Steidl
Düstere Str. 4 / 37073 Göttingen, Germany
Phone +49 551 49 60 60
mail@steidl.de
steidl.de

ISBN 978-3-96999-175-6
Printed in Germany by Steidl

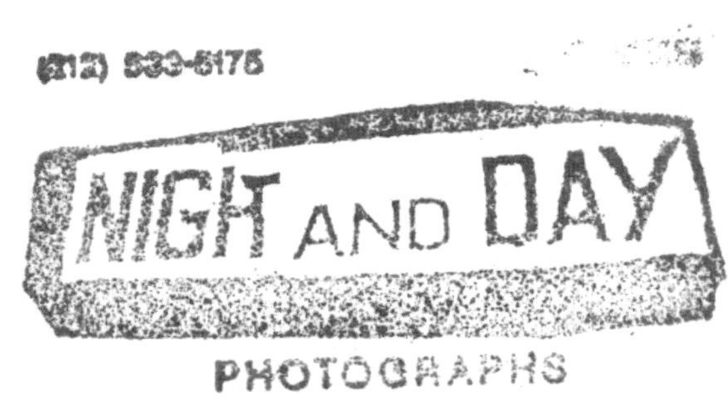